Growing Up Coastal
Life on the Georgia Coast

BY CLAY SIKES

DORRANCE
PUBLISHING CO
EST. 1920
PITTSBURGH, PENNSYLVANIA 15238

Dorrance Publishing Co
585 Alpha Drive
Pittsburgh, PA 15238
Visit our website at *www.dorrancebookstore.com*

ISBN: 978-1-6376-4038-8
eISBN: 978-1-6376-4885-8

Author Clay Sikes

Contact @ clay@thesikesgroup.com

Illustrations by Chris Walker
Contact @ cnwalkerdesigns@gmail.com

Dedicated to

my wife, Tracy – To My Children, Slade, Brett, and Ali.

Table of Contents

Growing Up Coastal

Life on the Georgia Coast

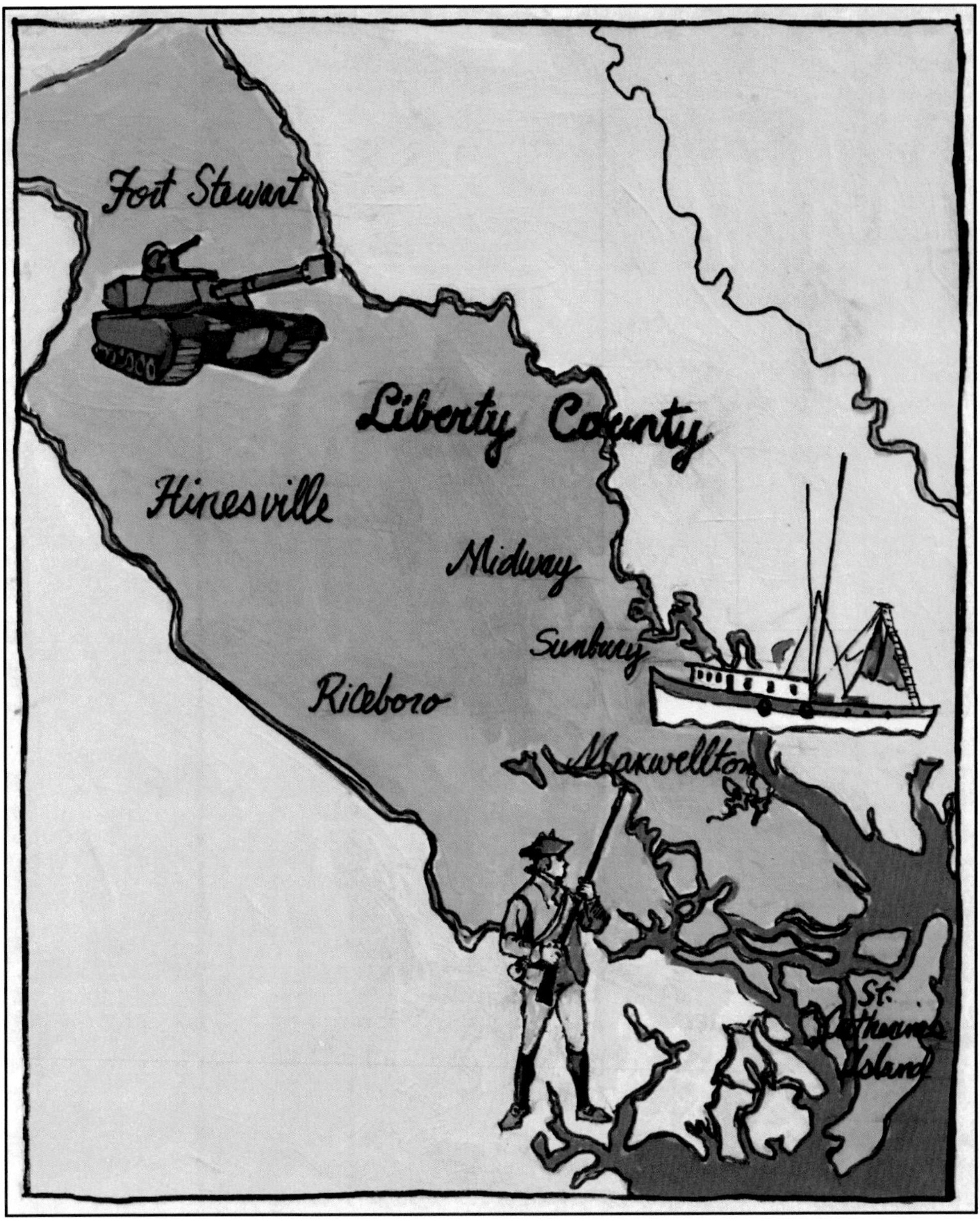
Fort Stewart
Liberty County
Hinesville
Midway
Sunbury
Riceboro
Maxwellton
St.
Island

1) Stories of Coastal Georgia

My life is filled with memories—a bank from which I make withdrawals, some of which I share here. Memories smile and frown as they flicker through my mind, producing joy and sadness all at the same time. A treasure is stored...I am never bored as I reflect, reject, and select what I want. Like jukebox songs, the tunes are what I choose, whether I win or lose, leap for joy, or cry out loud—memories, the stuff life is made of. I reflect back in time.

I have often been questioned about growing up as the son and grandson of high-sheriffs in rural, coastal Georgia. If asked to describe this in a single word, it would be "stories." You see, the high-sheriff is an elected office that calls for a dose of county politics mixed with demands of law enforcement. High drama can and did evolve in both arenas in the half-century of their service, yet the greatest overall drama was the change that came during these years.

Some of the narratives shared here relate to the sheriff's office; others don't—the common denominator being unique and memorable experiences of an ordinary life in a special place during a time of great change—the Georgia Coast.

Some stories have been tamed to be told for a variety of reasons, and in some cases, names are not mentioned as some aspects of these accounts aren't proud moments. Enemies, friends, law breakers, and law abiders created dozens of stories spanning the lengthy service of my father and grandfather, coupled with my own years of growing up coastal. My family became inextricably involved in a variety of events in the county as the role of rural sheriff journeyed beyond simple law enforcement to include peacemaker, provider, referee, enforcer, confidant, consultant, friend, and enemy. Even as children, we were held responsible, or given credit, for decisions (positive or negative) made by our grandfather and later, our father. Some hated us undeservedly just as others loved us undeservedly. As a child, it always mystified me how adults occasionally treated us as grownups.

At an early age, my brothers and I developed street sense about situations around us, and we often assumed responsibilities to help those that needed our help. As stated, a small-town sheriff, in those days, was much more than a leading law enforcement officer, as often what he dealt with we dealt with, even so in later years. If some thug put a hit on him, which happened, it rolled over on us, as we received warnings from the GBI (Georgia Bureau of Investigation) that our family may be car bombed. We had to check vehicles daily for several weeks until the danger passed. When he won a hard-fought election, it was as if we too had won. If he caught a bad guy, we too were credited, or so it seemed.

We were born and raised in Liberty County, an extremely unique location in that it is one of six counties comprising 113 miles of Atlantic coastline. It is home to Ft. Stewart, a sprawling army base, bookended by the port cities of Savannah to the north and Brunswick to the south. Situated next to Henry Ford's former playground, Bryan County, R.J. Reynolds's Sapelo Retreat in wild and wooly McIntosh County, and our own E.J. Nobles, owner of St. Catherine's Island, Life Saver Mints, and ABC Paramount, among other things.

Perhaps you begin to see the ingredients of this land of many stories when you weigh in on the unmatched characteristics and geography of Liberty County—miles of shoreline, low country river plantations, beautiful secluded barrier islands with miles of dunes and beaches, inland rivers upon which now "dead cities" evolved, all contributing to Liberty County's rich history—two signers of the Declaration of Independence, Revolutionary War battles, Civil War skirmishes, a port that rivaled Savannah—deepest natural harbor east of the Mississippi, gorgeous rivers leading to the Atlantic, and the largest military reservation east of the Mississippi—286,000 acres. All these inimitable characteristics blend to create a scene for many dramatic situations that I both witnessed and experienced.

The unusual combination of a rural coastal environment on the east end of the county, with a sprawling military complex on the west, made our rural lifestyle different from other agriculturally based small towns in the southeastern US. Saltwater and soldiers make life in Liberty unparalleled as small southeastern towns go—an agriculturally based community with an ocean and the army. Add to the mix social upheaval, the Civil Rights Movement, riots, assassinations, the constant threat of nuclear attack, emerging drug culture, generation gaps, and Southern rock music. As Bob Dylan so eloquently explained, the times were changing!

These stories primarily stem from experiences representing a slice of culture and history of Liberty County and Coastal Georgia circa 1960-2000. These forty years saw unprecedented change in race relations, as I vividly recall colored and white water fountains, bathrooms, recreation areas, and sadly, wretched discrimination. I loved a great grandmother who never saw a motorized vehicle until she was twenty. This same great grandma witnessed a man step onto the moon. I saw manufacturing of moonshine give way to growing marijuana as the primary source of underground commerce, smuggling become a way of life for many local shrimpers, African Americans become a force in local politics, Interstate 95 replace overburdened Highway 17, ending roadside motels, clip joints, and pecan shops. Change—incredible change was in the air.

I witnessed exploding residential growth in Hinesville, and ultimately in nearby Richmond Hill, as the sleepy little towns sprung to life with the activation of the 24th Infantry Division in 1974, creating thousands of jobs, new businesses, and economic opportunity. Our small town of a few thousand became a city of thousands almost overnight.

With so much cultural and economic change came challenge—challenge to adapt, to grow, and to change with the time. In many ways, we were like a cowboy town of the Wild West with smugglers on the coast and entrepreneurs in the city. Drugs and the counter-culture of the late sixties became a form of mainstream mindset in the seventies. Things were happening fast, and I was there to see it and to some extent experience it—the growth, the change, and memories from the past. I wasn't a saint; I experienced a lot of what was going on.

These stories are highlights from those years. Some, very personal: I debated telling them, yet leaving them out would be to shortchange the purpose of this chronicle, to record a piece of ordinary history about an ordinary life in Liberty County during an important time in our county and our country's history. Like Jackson Browne, in '69 I was twenty-one, a baby boomer ready to boom!

I have written much over the years, recording events as they happened. Some were written after the fact, as their memory etched deeply in me. In this book, I share what it was like growing up coastal in one of the most dynamic times in our nation's history. When done, there won't be much you won't know about me, or at least my past. As with everything, I've changed: most notably by and through my deep relationship with my Lord.

The short stories that follow are immediate strong points in my memory; many are centered around people: people I loved, respected, and who influenced who I am today. Growing up coastal was the thrill of my life; living here now is a dream come true.

2) Arrived – November 2019

Well, at long last, we're back here at Maxwellton, where we've sought to be for many years. You see, my new home, which I always thought would be home, just never seemed to work out...circumstances prevented it time and again. Now that I'm here, I want to tell you about my new alarm clock. In fact, it's called "sunrise in the face!" Though early, it's all right to be splashed with the sun—we face Van Dyke Creek and a beautiful barrier island, St. Catherines. The fresh morning air, having been sifted by thousands of miles of ocean, is sweet and pure. Breathing it is to breathe life, a renewal of sorts.

We're not settled yet, still living out of boxes, but it takes a while to unpack forty years in one place. As sad as leaving was, the excitement of being home is greater. In fact, it is surreal if not almost unbelievable. To have a dream and finally, approaching seventy-two, be here, a place so deeply loved by my ancestors, simply overwhelms me. The fact that it is stunning and beautiful is a big bonus. Nowhere I look do I not have a childhood memory. My mind is flooded with happy days with departed friends and family. I can walk down a road and another lost memory comes flooding back. Go to the riverbank and again, a flood of happy times...and the sound, the sound of silence—no highways, hustle and bustle—just the sound of the breeze in the palms, and marsh hens settling in the miles of open marsh grass.

Life is filled with many disappointments and heartbreaking defeat, but every once in a while, a bone is tossed, a shot of life—changing, unexpected joy that only God can give. This is that for me, a shot of life-changing, unexpected joy, that only God can give! My memories are flooded...I write to and for any audience who can relate to such times.

3) Memories of the Coastal Kind

The howl of marsh hens waffled across the Salt River, as early morning sun shot shivers of color into my waking eyes. Rising sun, a spectacular parade of coastal light, can hardly be matched in sheer beauty. My head throbbed, my body wet from the dew of darkness, yet even this discomfort could not deny the excitement of sunrise on the coast. Others slept around what remained of a campfire, but a new day was happening, and youthful energy filled my body. What to do? Life on the coast offered plenty, and plans were spontaneous in 1964—St. Catherine's, Ossabaw, Blackbeard, islands of adventure. Crab, shrimp, fish? Maybe an early beer from Tippins, fried shrimp at the Lodge, and those Savannah girls will be at Half Moon tonight. We'll see what the day brings.

Fifty years later, standing on the same spot of ground, memories flood my mind. I can clearly see the embers of the campfire, my sleeping buddies, and the sun's spectacle rising above the barrier island. Where has time gone? How did fifty years go by? I can still feel the throb in my head—too much watered-down beer, the kind we bought on nearby Ft. Stewart. There we lay, sleeping on the ground without a blanket, teenage boys with a belly full of beer and a ton of life to live—yet I blink and fifty years. On the riverbank, arms folded, mind reflecting, I sense the same sounds, sights, and oneness with nature a half plus century later. Many things have changed, but some never do. Life, what a trip!

Summer nights at Half Moon bring its transient population home, lights identifying the many families in summer residence. The Half Moon river creates a semicircle of homes clearly evident for a two-mile sphere. Summer friends were seen but once a year in the days and nights of summer in the mood and celebration of vacation.

The warmth of an embrace from a day on the coast is memorable—those who get to enjoy it as a lifestyle are truly favored. Geography relates to what warms our soul. Time will take us all, but this beauty will remain, or at least, I hope it does. The Georgia Coast is alluring—it is good for making memories! And, we had a blast at Half Moon!

4) Kindness from a Stranger
– Winter 1960

The bow of a boat on a cold predawn morning is no place to be, unless that boat is heading to "no place you'd rather be." The 'Laura Lee,' the island boat, was making its morning voyage back to the island from the mainland, and of greater importance, I was on it. The old men and adults were huddled in the warm cabin, the work hands on the stern, but the bow was just fine for me and the other equally excited youngsters. The freezing cold air had us shaking with excitement as we were soon to live out a dream. The morning sun peeped ever so slightly as we arrived at the main island dock.

Finally, my years of waiting were over; in a few short minutes, my feet would be on St. Catherine's Island for the first time, and of even greater importance, to hunt deer. Most of my young life was filled with stories of this mysterious island; it's sheer beauty and bounty in deer. I had heard of parties attended by Edward J. Nobles, R.J. Reynolds, Sheriffs Poppell and Sikes, gifts given to locals including my own family by them, some of the wealthiest men of their era. Stories of deer hunts where virtually everyone kills a deer. What could be more exciting for a young hunter?

All the stories would now come to life, and now I would have one of my own. And tonight, I'd spend the night in the home of a signer of the Declaration of Independence, Button Gwinnett; I would see the giant fireplace I heard so much about and feel its warmth—lay my head where titans of industry and movie fame slept. Eat food prepared for a king, smell Cuban cigars, and listen to stories from statewide political luminaries. Nothing could excite a south Georgia twelve-year-old more!

Another treat to me was meeting Bobby Russell, nephew to Senator Richard B. Russell. Our family already bore connection to the Russells, as my mother's dad, many years before, was college roommates with the future senator. I was oblivious to this at the time. Years later, I had a meeting in Senator Saxby Chambless's office in the "Richard B. Russell Building" in DC, only then really recognizing the importance of the past and the Russell name.

Every expectation I had of the island was exceeded, as the first day was spent touring with dignitaries in tow. Governor Earnest Vandiver killed a deer or three, which were prepared for the evening meal. The governor had known my grandfather, and seemed fond of my dad, riding in a Jeep and spending much time with him during the two-day hunt. Other statewide officials were there, all seeming to have a good time...seems someone brought a large jug of white corn whisky. Our second night was almost without sleep for us "beyond excited" youngsters as we were all paired in one room. Tomorrow, we would hunt! I might kill my first deer; in fact I knew I would—the deer were far too plentiful for me not to. I remember thinking like a kid at Christmas, this could be the night before I kill my first deer. The night passed fast, and soon the "wake bell" rung, and breakfast served. We were then assigned to island Jeeps with other hunters to take an assigned stand. It was here I first met Mr. Bobby Russell, who would be standing next to me the entire hunt. As we rode to our stands, he asked if ever I had killed a deer. At age twelve, I was almost ashamed to tell him no. I knew he was related to somebody my St. Simons granddaddy knew, somebody important, but little else did I know about him or his family.

The morning drive was filled with action with much shooting around me, but I saw nothing. When we gathered for lunch, I learned Mr. Bobby had killed two, and each of the other youngsters had too killed deer. Mr. Bobby could read disappointment on my face, encouraging me the afternoon hunt would bring good fortune, and it did with a fine seven point. I had finally killed my first deer—a big relief for a young deer hunter. I wore the traditional blood smear proudly, not wanting to leave my deer to be taken away and cleaned. I at least wanted the horns, the trophy we young hunters desire most.

Soon it was time to board the Laura Lee for the return voyage to the St. Catherine's dock at Half Moon on Colonel's Island. It seemed everyone had horns to go with the generous portion of meat each hunter received, but my seven point was nowhere to be found. I was thrilled to have my first ever deer but heartbroken to have nothing to show for it. My daddy encouraged me to get on the boat and not complain about it. Just maybe the horns would show up in the future. What the heck did he mean by that? Only one thing beats having the horns of your first deer, and that is having the full head mounted, but what twelve-year-old could afford that?

Just as the Laura Lee, an old converted shrimp boat, entered the North Newport River heading to Half Moon, Daddy beckoned me to the cabin where he and Mr. Bobby were talking. He said, "The reason you didn't get your horns back on the island is because your new friend, Mr. Bobby Russell, is paying to have your deer mounted. You'll have it in about two months."

I was floored; I think a tear or two rolled down my face. I couldn't thank Mr. Bobby enough. Somehow, he knew what that mount meant to me, and though he had not known me, his measured act of kindness touched me deeply. I will never forget. Strangely, I never saw him again, but I never forgot the extreme kindness he showed an excited twelve-year-old boy. That head hung on the most prominent part of our Maxwellton house wall from 1960 to 2012 when the house was renovated. I have played it forward many times, just as Mr. Bobby had done for me, keeping this act of kindness alive as long as I am, hoping others do the same.

RIP Mr. Bobby Russell, you and your generous act of kindness will never be forgotten!

5) The Puma-Cat – Summer 1962

In the summer of 1962, I was a spry fourteen-year-old who loved the coast so much I invented ways to stay on it. You see, we lived in the same county as our coastal home, but thirty-three miles away in Hinesville. Our family land and home on Colonel's Island at Maxwellton afforded me this unusual opportunity. Maxwellton, named for its original owner, was granted lands by the king of England. These lands offered us mystery, intrigue, great hunting, fishing, and pure beauty. Our family was the fourth generation to own it since the original king's grant.

In order to spend a whole summer on the coast, I had to find something that my parents would find acceptable. The only possibility of being allowed to live here was to find work. I loved the water, and working on it was my ultimate goal. Even as a child, I found crabbing a fascinating lifestyle; many, like their shrimping counterparts, spent winters in Key West and spring and summers here. I always thought it cool that folks could live in two places in the same year, following the shrimp and crabs. We saw them for five or six months, and then they went back to Key West. Crabs are plentiful in the warm months on the Georgia Coast, full of meat, and in-demand...and I wanted in!

My plan was to buy fifty traps from J.W. Morgan, who also bought my crabs, piece together an old crab boat and used motor hand-cranked by rope. The challenges were many, but my determination to go into business and prove I could accomplish my greater goal—living on Maxwellton and being on the water—was my ultimate objective. Profit was not my motive, and that proved to be a good thing; breaking even was all I ever accomplished, but living all summer on the island was my prize.

Putting this together began in the winter as I began the search for equipment to launch my summer on the river. I had a short span of time, until the first week in August, because I was committed to high school football. I would jump it in early June and get two full months of pulling traps, maybe make enough to pay them off in my first year. My old boat leaked, and my motor had to be started eight or ten times by rope during my fifty-trap run. I hand pulled each trap, loading the heavy weighted trap full of crabs into an upright drum. I often filled two and occasionally three 55-gallon drums with crab. My next challenge was getting them loaded from the boat to the dock, then down the dock, then into the back of our occasionally running family Jeep, and then to Morgan's Shrimp and Crab dock six or seven miles away at Sunbury. My human powered hoist had to be hooked into the 55-gallon drums, lifted manually, then swung back and to until there was enough momentum to get the heavy drum over the dock, then dropped at just the right time. This always resulted in crabs falling all over the dock, which I caught by hand and returned to the barrel. My hands were often bloody from being bitten; I never wore gloves for any of this work…and don't ask me why, but I was strong, adapted to the heat, and was ready for football.

Getting my traps properly situated with currents, baiting techniques, and finding great spots to place them fell to my friend Toby Roberts. Toby crabbed for the Morgan family and had been a long-time friend to our family; his knowledge and experience was invaluable in getting me started. His advice gave me some chance of succeeding. He taught me how to "bait-up," letting my frozen fish thaw at the end of the dock, then stringing my bait strings with fish before daylight, readying them for the traps when crabs were emptied into the barrels. It is here that this story really begins.

At about the two-week mark, my routine was beginning to unfold: Rise at or before daylight, string my now thawed-out fish strategically placed at the end of the dock (purchased the day before from Morgan's Shrimp and Crab Dock), gas up, and hit the river. An early start was critical as the intense heat and humidity were draining. Daily, I pulled fifty traps, pulled the engine hand rope eight or ten times, loaded crabs into drums and unloaded them at Sunbury, bought bait (frozen fish), and returned home for a much needed rest. I had no help in my earliest days of crabbing, so my daddy was curious enough to actually come down and spend the night with me, checking out my work and routine. This kind of attention was a bit unusual, so naturally I was thrilled he was there, taking an interest in me living my dream.

He arrived a bit late, but time enough to eat some crab with me. I ate a lot of crab that summer. The plan was to stay the night, get up, and see me off to work my lines. I slept a little later than normal, but as always, I walked onto the screened porch facing the dock and river and dressed. Daylight was happening fast, and Daddy was still asleep, so I would dress fast and get him up to see me off…but something was soon to happen that would create years of fear and excitement all rolled into one.

This morning would greet me with the most unexpected surprise, and then I saw it! What I was seeing was so odd that my mind couldn't grasp it, yet the light was enough to see it clearly, only a hundred or so feet away. What I saw I have never seen since—a giant cat so big and majestic, light brown (almost tan) in color, who should be on a mountain top out west, not down here on the Georgia Coast on my dock! His long tail pointed up as he helped himself to my now mushy unfrozen bait fish. He looked like a hungry dog who hadn't been fed for a long time. I watched him in steely silence, mesmerized at the sight of something so beautiful and unusual feasting in our backyard. I blinked and squinted to make sure of what I was seeing.

I got to get my daddy up, he has got to see this!

I quietly stepped away, entering my sleeping dad's room. I woke him, telling him he must see what I'd just seen on the end of the dock. He groggily jumped from bed, rushing to the porch, but no cat! He was gone, and Daddy was a bit perturbed at being awakened so suddenly. I plead my case, "Daddy, you cannot believe how big this cat is."

He responded that I'd seen nothing more than a common bobcat. My heart sank. I knew what I'd seen was no bobcat, but how could I convince him I saw something that didn't exist in these parts? He walked with me to examine the bait. It was clear something of size had been in my fish, but not convincing enough.

In the days following this incident, I asked island old timers about such a cat; no one had ever seen or heard of such. I drove to town that weekend to look up what I saw in our encyclopedias. I was shocked to see a similar cat described as a mountain lion or puma. Then, my story was even more unbelievable as no such cats live in these parts, but I knew what I'd seen. This birthed a frustration in me.

As August approached, my summer of crabbing was over until next year. I stored my traps and worn out boat and motor with every intention of returning for my fifteenth year of summer. My motor would have to be replaced, but I had time to figure that out. Football now had my full attention, but my frustration remained very strong until early fall when my dad's friend and electrician, Carl White, came to the coast to do some work. He too saw this cat, describing him much the same as I did. Mr. Carl White was just as amazed as I was at his unusually large size. The cat jumped in the road in front of him, providing a great view and paw print. Now my daddy believed me! Further evidence came a few months later when a young calf from our herd was caught, killed, and dragged several hundred yards and eaten under Charles Jones's boat house. Interestingly, only his back was eaten out, the rest of his body untouched. Whether intended that way or too spooked to leave his prey, we don't know.

Soon after, his tracks were seen often—his paw of uncommon size for even the largest of bobcats. We also saw evidence of claw sharpening high up on leaning trees; so high a grown man could stand with his hands lifted to touch the marks. The cat spooked us. Had it escaped from some circus, now so old it must take domesticated animals? Would humans be next? Needless to say, this made night coon hunts at Maxwellton scary and often humorous.

Three African American guys that worked with us in the family oil business loved to coon hunt, often without dogs. We would hunt on moonless nights, finding coons in trees by headlight. This required deep walks in very dark woods. On this night, my brother Steve, Eddie Lee Gaulden, Willie Joe, and A.L. Quarterman hunted from a single truck parked out on a nearby road. Somehow we packed five men in an old single seat work truck. Discussion of the cat arose as we all were uncomfortable that something of unknown origin roamed these woods.

Any sound set us off, but the shrieking shrill of a screaming cat put us to flight. Who knows whether from a common bobcat or the big cat himself such a scream occurred! And five men logged jammed the shotgun side of the pickup truck. We literally logged jammed, meaning we couldn't get in or out—a mass of ass all arrived at the same piece of real estate at the same time! By then, we were laughing so hard (at ourselves) that the cat could've caught and eaten us all. We relived this moment on many occasions, producing the same roar raucous laughter amongst ourselves and any we told.

The puma cat didn't catch us that night, nor was he seen or heard from again for many years. Signs of him, or one like him, showed up on roads and tree scrapes, but no one I know saw him again. To this day, we are unsure; some telling us it was nothing more than a light furred Florida panther, yet panthers don't match the size of what I saw. Others reports of seeing big cats on the coast have come in recent years in nearby counties. I too saw what appeared to be a Florida panther while returning from a hunting trip to nearby Dorchester Quail.

Whatever it was, we still called it "the puma cat," and thus began the big cat legend that still lives on the Georgia Coast.

6) An Island Misadventure – Summer 1962

A hot July night was cooled by an ocean breeze skipping off a high spring tide; the island's darkness illuminated by a beaming full moon. Crickets and whippoorwills sang summer tunes as darting shadows silhouetted my bedroom walls, making monsters of blowing moss on swaying oak limbs. Windows were never closed in 1960s remote island cottages—the evening air was cooler than a cottage consumed in coastal humidity. Every outside sound and movement eerily lived within the few homes occupying the remote coastal island. In the 1960s, air conditioning was rare, and even more rare on the remote islands of Georgia, yet this was my summer home with its unprecedented privacy, isolated beaches, towering dunes, high bluffs, and refreshing ocean breezes. Plus, I had access to my own Jeep, island house, dock, boat, and all the beer a teenager could drink while avoiding the troubles of more populated areas. Isolated islands were void of public highways and people (unless invited). I liked it that way.

Traditionally, my teenage summers were spent roaming the coast, bouncing from island to island in search of new adventure. Various friends joined me in this incredible lifestyle, and like all youngsters, we had our spots, our favorite island or beach, carefully selected according to the day's plan that included drinking, discovering, sunning, swimming, fishing, girls, and occasionally a party (or two). We strayed onto civilized islands like Tybee, St.

Simons, or Jekyll, but only if something special was happening. Our real hangout were barrier islands with names like Black Beard, Ossabaw, Sapelo, and St. Catherine's.

As previously stated, I had to work in the summer, and my job was conveniently chosen such that I could live on my beloved coast. At fourteen, I became a professional crabber, pulling fifty crab traps with an under-powered motor that actually worked but had to be hand-roped, restarted eight or ten times to power me through my 50-trap run. Through two summers, I barely made any money, financing traps and buying gas and oil from the dock master who also bought my crabs. My lowly fifty traps barely yielded enough to pay the bills, but I didn't really care—I was living where I wanted to be, doing what I wanted to do, and having a ball! I seldom left the island, once staying almost the entire summer without returning to town. Isolation scared me a little, but I loved it more—a paradoxical aspect of my personality.

Some years prior to my birth, my grandfather purchased a big chunk of the eastern side of Colonel's Island, a genuine low country river plantation called Maxwellton, named for one of its former owners, the Maxwell family. As kids, growing up on this land was special. We recognized, even as small children, that we were extremely fortunate to enjoy such a heritage. We are only the fourth family to own it since the original grant from the king of England. This land had once served as a working plantation supporting wealthy planters from a bygone era, and now provided a Mecca for the entire Sikes family. Thursday evening fish suppers, mullet jumping, hunting, fishing, and social gatherings were regular events for sixty years.

Even as a young teenager, I wasn't afraid to be one of the few inhabitants on the island, but at times, during the night, I battled lonely fear that would almost paralyze me. I think I liked the challenge of conquering my fear, and staying alone on long summer nights satisfied that. I would awaken the next morning like I had done something special, glad for my brave accomplishment. Since early childhood, I had heard all the old ghost stories, mostly from the few remaining children and grandchildren of slaves who lived in the area; all about Voodoo, haints, sea creatures, pirates, and modern-day smugglers who supposedly made their presence known on the islands. This added to making isolated island living exciting, but also extremely frightening at times for a fourteen-year-old. This night would prove to be just that—frightening, and justifiably so! It is etched in my memory forever.

Our island home, formerly an old oyster processing plant, faced east, providing a visual connect with traffic in the Intracoastal waterway, and a direct easterly view of St. Catherine's, Ossabaw, Black Beard, and Sapelo Islands. We can see into three counties while standing in the fourth. Where else but the mountains can you do that? Maxwellton is chocked full of artifacts, including Indian and plantation era relics. We never lacked for something to do, and our early love of hunting was satisfied by boundless amounts of wild game—deer, raccoon, squirrel, and wild hog, and a fox hunter's delight in the early years when fox hunting was still popular. I spent every day possible on this plantation, and my earliest stories of coastal Georgia begin here, in the summer of 1962.

As I stared at the shadows being cast against my front bedroom wall, against the backdrop of rising moonlight, I kept thinking I saw something of human form coming out of the river. I told myself, "You are seeing things...quit scaring the crap out of yourself with your wild imagination!" As hard as I tried to not see the reflection of a human silhouette amongst the wildly waving moss, the fact remained: I was seeing something I had never witnessed. It was a man, or an ape, or something really big, and it was walking upright toward the house. I kept thinking that my mind was really playing tricks on me—that's just blowing moss flailing in the strong ocean breeze!

I could no longer justify the image out of my mind. I was seeing an undeniable man-form coming from the river walking toward the house.

I was frozen—never been this afraid before! There was no phone or gun, yet this unknown creature was coming into the yard, and maybe even toward my window. I ducked under the cover in hopes I was dreaming or just seeing things, yet when I looked again, the incredibly large creature was standing near the house and my window. I tried to muster up a scream, but just like in a dream, nothing came out but my breath. I was literally frightened beyond words. I was going to be consumed by some sea monster nobody ever heard of, and likely nobody would know what happened to me!

As I lay there shivering, I waited for sure death. Would I be eaten alive? Carried down to the murky depths of some ocean, or just killed right where I lay? The level of fear that gripped me was intense. Was this the end? Would my life end in a mystery no one would unravel? Why was a creature standing in my yard? My heart pounded through my chest. And then it hit me—I still had one remaining option! I could run; I would run like the freaking wind! In fact, I could probably run all the way to Midway, the closest thing to civilization at that time, and if this "thing" could catch me...well, he deserved to eat me! Renewed hope came from the normal emotional response that hits in times of great fear—fight or flight, and flight was now in full gear.

No sooner had the thought hit me that adrenalin flooded my body, providing a surge of explosive energy. I was on my feet, scrambling for the door. I knew I had to escape the front bedroom that faced the river, make my way to the back of the house, and out the back door before Sasquatch could come around to the front. With one bound, I was at the bedroom door, which occasionally would lock you inside the bedroom for no apparent reason (and had to be opened from the outside). Surely, this would not be one of those occasions, and thank the Lord it wasn't. Otherwise, my hand or the doorknob would have come off that night! I covered about thirty feet in three steps as one remaining door was all between me and a death-defying escape. It seemed like it took forever, but I unbolted the big wooden door at the back, and as I reached for the screen door about to marathon to Midway, I caught movement out of the corner of my left eye. The full moon revealed that the monster had heard my commotion and circled the house into the front yard to intercept me.

As I pushed the screen door open, I saw my nemesis rounding the corner into the front yard coming into full view of my retreat path.

I can still run, and he will have to catch me, I thought.

Just as I took flight, I heard my named called. "Mr. Sikes! Is that you Mr. Sikes?" In those days, particularly on the islands, older African Americans often addressed young whites as "Mister." I didn't like it, as I was surely no mister. Though I didn't know the voice, I immediately recognized the Geechee brogue of an older black man—the dialect of the coastal regions of Georgia and South Carolina. This Cajun pattern of speech has passed through generations of white and black families alike, the common thread being linkage to the coast. I stopped cold in my tracks as I was relieved, yet at the same time remorseful at the sound of this gentle giant known as Roosevelt Moran. Immediately, I knew why he had paid me a visit, and I knew I had brought this unpleasantness upon myself.

You see, Roosevelt had run crab lines as long as anyone could remember. His lines and my lines ran opposite sides of the river, and we respected each other's territory, even though I was the new kid on the block. Someone continuously robbed my traps, especially the ones nearest Roosevelt's. I was told, and ignorantly believed, that Roosevelt was stealing my hard-earned crabs, and like the juvenile delinquent I was, I stuffed a sealed bottle in one of his traps with a shotgun shell inside stating, "The next one will be for you if you steal any more of my crabs." My shameful act toward an honorable man dictated a face-to-face visit, no matter the hour.

Roosevelt let me know that he had never taken anyone's crabs though he often suffered theft at the hands of river thieves who abounded in that era. My earlier fright turned into regret and deep disgust at my immature actions. All I could do was deeply apologize for my unbridled and uncalled-for behavior. Roosevelt lived in neighboring McIntosh County, and though I had heard of him, I really didn't know him until that night. His visit at such an untimely hour threw me off, but as he explained in our fortuitous meeting, "Nothing more important, Mr. Sikes, than talking when people threatening 'bout killing one another." I agreed.

I later saw Roosevelt many times on the river and on land. He pulled my boat with its malfunctioning motor to my dock on several occasions. He also gave me advice about setting my traps. He was well respected for his vast knowledge of the river and the honorable man he was. I was happy to call him friend, and I will never forget the night we met.

7) Father Knows Best

"Two things you must never do, son: allow your shotgun to fall in the dirt or put your hands on a wounded deer," said Bobby Sikes to his young son. Many lessons on gun and hunting safety were drilled into our young heads long before we ever carried a shotgun on an organized hunt. Why would I ever throw my gun in the dirt, or even get near a wounded deer? Never, I thought! I'd heard tales of dangerous deer hooves...even bringing death to unfortunates who encountered a wounded or dying deer.

Deer hunting at Maxwellton always hosted the same folks and same old traditions. Gathering early at the front gate, planning the hunt, dispersing standers to different roads, standing at prearranged distances, awaiting dogs to find deer scent and get on a chase. A pack of dogs finding their trained smell initiates the excitement. Deer are much faster, and often smarter, than their pursuers. The big bucks use water, giant leaps in another direction, and wind to out-fox, outmaneuver, and survive. Extremely thick foliage in this part of the country makes hunting these woods difficult, hence the dogs. The marsh is another great advantage for deer in coastal dog hunting.

As the day wound down, older men always hovered at the front gate, talking about the day's hunt, things in general, and maybe a nip from the bottle under the seat. On cold days, maybe several nips and a little more talk, even a fire to stand around as the dog men drove the roads, looking for straggling or lost dogs. This was the least exciting part for us young ones. Too young to drink and banter with the old guys, we often hung out with our own talk.

Just such was the scene in 1962 at the Maxwellton gate. Late in the day, freezing cold, yet off in the far distance, my friend, Danny Goodman, and I heard the faint sound of a single dog hot on the trail. "Seems to be heading toward the dirt road we're at the end of," I told Danny. Without much fanfare, we slipped away, allowing the old folks to continue their day's end enjoyment. As we got further down the road, the faint sound grew louder and closer to our dirt road, and we quickened our pace. By the dog's sound and angle, we thought the deer would cross way ahead of where we were. We began to run, me up front and Danny behind. Suddenly, the sound stopped...maybe the dog lost the scent of the deer, maybe it was one of those wily bucks who could slip a dog with great skill. Silence, but we kept walking briskly just in case. I remembered I only had the three shells in my gun, the extras already unloaded in Daddy's truck.

Suddenly, now a good half mile from the gate, the dog opened again, sounding much like he was close and right on top of us on the dirt road. It was getting dark but still light enough to see a deer sneak to the road's edge. I trembled, heart pounding, wide-eyed, knowing something big was about to happen, likely Danny or I would get a chance at this deer.

Hope it's a buck, I thought. Does were off limits at Maxwellton in those days, so only horns would do. As soon as the thought left my head, horns appeared, standing still and very quiet behind some brush a few steps from the road. I actually saw his horns before I saw the rest of him blending so well in the sage, much closer to me than Danny. I lifted my granddaddy's Remington Automatic, firing all three loads of buckshot into the grand old buck. He was still standing in the same place but quivered with each shot. Though he didn't fall, I knew he was hit.

I looked to Danny, but he was a bit far to shoot, so I settled in my mind this big fellow wasn't getting away as I'd seen happen many times. As I turned back to my buck, he was turning back to the woods, and yes, I threw my empty gun to the ground, determined not to let this wounded buck get away. He ran, and I ran after him. As the eight point began climbing a small hill at the wood's edge, he stumbled just enough for me to jump on his back, grab his horns in an effort to get him down.

My death grip on his horns allowed him to easily toss me over his head. I hit the ground hard on my back on the opposite side and bottom of the hill.

The buck stood above me, rising slightly up on his hind feet with hoofs pointed downward toward me. Before I could think what to do next, Danny Goodman came quickly and bravely through the woods, hitting this now dangerous animal with his knife. Blood was everywhere. Adrenalin flowed as the now dying deer lay next to me. Danny, my savior, stood in shock at what just happened! Danny was brave; I was stupid!

Though there was great merit in killing a big buck, I now had to face my daddy for violating his number one hunting rule: "Don't ever put your hands on a wounded deer." Hearing the commotion, he had quickly driven down Maxwellton Road to our location, where he saw his daddy's old gun in the dirt. He was mad, mad as hell, and paid little attention that Danny and I were pulling a big buck from the wood's edge, much less what happened in those woods to kill it. I gladly took my butt chewing about the gun, hoping little or no info would ever surface about how the deer was killed.

Danny and I kept the events of that day quiet for several years until one day Daddy overheard me telling the story of Danny's bravery. He popped his head in the room and said, "Damn good thing I didn't know that then!"

8) Front Porch Justice – 1960s

Back in the 60s, domestic violence was a big problem, even more so with poor families. This problem was exacerbated by laws that invariably favored males, often at the expense of females. Without hard evidence of an attack, there was little law enforcement could or would do—it was more "he said, she said." Again, this system favored men when the predominate number of officers were men in a favored system. Without hard evidence of abuse, prosecution was difficult.

Without blood, bad bruises, or an open wound, officers were hard-pressed to make a case. Fortunately, laws drastically changed, and domestic violence crimes are being treated fairly and aggressively as they should, but back then, things were different.

In rural areas in the 60s, it seemed everyone having an issue at night came to the sheriff's house, rang his doorbell, and waited for him to appear to air out their problem (right there on the front porch). As sheriff's kids, we saw it all. Our split-level home featured a suite of bedrooms upstairs, and ours overlooked the white marble-wrapped front porch. This was cool because we, being curious boys, could eavesdrop on sheriff business. We heard it all undetected—some of it was juicy, but mostly routine things a rural sheriff must deal with.

By reflex, when that doorbell rang in the middle of the night, we were there, peeping out the window, our nosy little selves lapping up the latest criminal info. The things we heard: stories, excuses, marriage issues, drunk talk, mamas crying for their always innocent sons, men mad at other men, cheating wives, cheating husbands, stealing, bribe offers from circus people, flim-flam men, con men, gamblers, pimps. This was an army town. You name it, it came to the big front door with the white marble porch.

While the front porch sheriff's office continued for years, nothing, and I mean nothing, prepared us for the night one visitor made the most lasting memory of all, one that haunts me to this day—a sight so horrific that the normal mind is incapable of imagining it!

If you guessed a 1,000 guesses, you would never imagine what arrived on our porch one school night just as Mother's bridge club was breaking up, a site so unimaginable that we couldn't believe our eyes. "Are we seeing what we think we see?"

You see, over several months, one black lady kept coming to our door complaining that her husband hit her, slapped her, hollered at her, but constantly, she was told there was not enough evidence to take a warrant for her abuser. Her trips to our door were many, but always to no avail. Then came a Thursday night when all that changed. She now had a head full of evidence, plain for all to see, confirmed by a white marble floor that soon turned red.

I've seen a lot in seven decades, but never have I seen a human being drive herself to a house, ring a doorbell with an ax stuck in the top of her head, just like in a lighter knot stump!

This lady banged on the doorbell screaming, "I got de ebidence now, Mr. Bobby! I got his ass now, Mr. Bobby!" My daddy wasn't home, but we knew a living room full of lady bridge players were about to get the shock of their lives! And when my mother opened the door to this lady screaming about "ebidence," the lady onlookers began gasping, even screaming, themselves. What a mess at 33 Timberlane Circle, as by now the white marble was covered in blood. My mama, a nurse, knew she had to get this lady to the hospital. The bridge ladies were screaming and the lady was screaming as the scene was one of great chaos.

By now, our town's only doctor, who lived across the street, heard the commotion and came running, telling the lady about the emergency room. He needed to get her there immediately. He planned to call an ambulance, but she thought he meant for her to drive there. Before we knew what was happening, she hopped in her car with the axe in her head and drove to the ER.

Watching her enter her car, crank it back it up, and drive to the ER was surreal, like a bad dream! I think we were in shock!

This crazy story has a happy ending as our town doc actually beat her to the ER and removed the ax successfully, from which she fully recovered. Though the sheriff missed all the commotion at his home, a house full of witnesses and a porch full of blood was enough evidence to send this man away.

Such were the ways back then...

9) The Hunted Hunter – 1962

It was a cold October morning in 1962, and the annual Green's Pasture/Sheriff's Hunt, a 50-year tradition on the Georgia coast in Liberty County, was in its first hour. Grits, cheese eggs, country-smoked sausage, and hot coffee had warmed our stomachs long before daylight on this uncharacteristically cold morning. Subfreezing temperatures had partially frozen the standing water in ditches and shallow ponds throughout the 6,000-acre plantation, the site of our yearly gathering.

Most of the hunt's usual cast of characters were in attendance, including Freeman Smith, a longtime friend of my deceased grandfather and well-known local hunter. Mr. Freeman had seen more hunts in Green's Pasture than anyone alive and knew the pasture like the back of his hand. Deer trails, deer crossings, feeding areas, and where the deer lay up during the day—he knew all.

As the hunt master's son, I had again skillfully elected to drive dogs with Mr. Freeman as opposed to taking the traditional road stand. At least in the woods, I could move around and follow my instincts, and more importantly, I knew Mr. Freeman's specific routine, including where he would release his well-trained pack of beagles.

In past years, his turnout spot had always produced the desired result— jumping a big buck! If my calculations were correct, based on past experience, he would jump his swift prey on the roadside of an existing cypress pond and proceed hastily to the marsh and eventually to the safety of one of the many marsh islands that dot the landscape in Green's Pasture. The hunt was considered by many to be a significant event in Liberty County. Invitations were coveted and often attracted luminaries from professional sports, politics, and big business. Invitees, however, were all treated the same; a Gum Branch farmer was just as important as a Hall of Fame baseball player, a U.S Congressman, or an Atlanta millionaire. The hunt's main purpose was for family, friends, and political supporters of my father and grandfather to gather together for fellowship and fun.

The scene was set. I hitched a ride ahead of Mr. Freeman and quickly positioned myself deep in the woods on the other side of the near frozen cypress pond. Finding my way through the dark woods, I was able to locate a huge live oak tree as my deer stand. The base of the tree stretched five or six feet and offered a perfect seat facing the cypress pond. In the distance, I soon heard the familiar and exciting sound of tailgates dropping, yielding the anxious hunting dogs as they entered the woods for the first time in a year. Hunting deer with dogs is limited to a very small portion of the nation's geography, with the dense forest of coastal Georgia having one of the richest traditions in the rarely given privilege. In this type hunting, surprise is the order of the day, and this day would prove to be no exception.

In the early 60s, hunting was taken seriously in Liberty County—many older hunters having grown up in an era when hunting was more necessity than sport. Rigid rules and traditions were obeyed and respected. As a result, standers were on their deer stands before or shortly after daylight, and dogs were turned out as soon as the first light provided visibility. Sound can be heard for miles, the canopy serving as a conduit, forcing the sound from the hunting dogs to be heard in many directions and far distances.

I nestled next to the large live oak, loaded my gun, and visually picked several spots across the cypress pond from which I expected the deer to run. My expectations were high when I heard Mr. Freeman in the distance begin his familiar, "Yiiiiip!! Yiiiiip!!" —an odd but familiar sound to hunting dogs and hunters alike. The sound of Mr. Freeman's voice excited his beagles, and they in turn began to yelp with their own excitement. I knew whatever good fortune the day held for me was about to happen. My heart began to pound, always a sign of excitement.

How proud and smart I felt outsmarting the wily buck. Did not, during the two prior years, dogs enter this same cypress pond area and jump a huge buck? Well, this year would be different; instead of the wise old buck escaping, as he normally did, I would intervene and cut off his escape route and probably kill the biggest deer on the hunt. Who knows, maybe the biggest of the entire season. This distinction, among teenage hunters of Liberty County, was a badge of great honor. This badge of horns could be worn for a long time, nailed to a tree or the back of a barn, often shown for years after the big day. Only the wisest of hunters could kill the big bucks, and even the older generation respected a fourteen-year-old who could kill a "big bucka," as they often called it.

As previously alluded to, surprise and its consequences make up the gist of this tale. It has not been told before—known only to God and myself. So please, upon reading and hopefully enjoying its content, forget you ever read such an embarrassing story! You see, as I sat quietly expecting to see the great "bucka" come running around or through the cypress pond from the direction I was facing, I was soon to encounter a great surprise.

Mr. Freeman's "yiiiip!" got louder as he approached the cypress pond, but he was still several hundred yards away and entering the exact area I expected to hear the first outburst from the dogs. Suddenly, all of Mr. Freeman's trained beagles were in full roar. The sound of ten or twelve deer dogs suddenly getting on the scent of a deer will produce an excitement in a young hunter that cannot be explained—the thrill of the kill, the badge of honor, respect from older hunters, and the marksmanship and pure hunting skill it takes to kill "the big one" all rolled into one experience! How could anything top this?

As the roar of the dogs' shrill voices became louder—a sign the deer was getting closer—my heart was literally pounding so hard I could hear it. Frozen in my spot next to the big oak, I pointed my grandfather's old 12-guage automatic shotgun in the general direction of the dogs' distant barks, and toward a clearing and trail next to the cypress pond. Deer usually run well ahead of the dogs, so I had to be ready.

My flashlight had revealed many deer tracks on this trail during my pre-dawn hike, and I had taken a position that allowed me to fire directly across the pond toward the small clearing. By now the sound of the dogs, hot on the trail, was deafening. The very still and cold morning intensified the exciting harmony of deer dogs on the first morning of hunting season. As the pack of dogs approached the trail leading to the cypress pond, instead of coming toward me and following the expected trail route, their direction turned to my immediate right. My eyes searched along the pond's edge where I spotted another trail, and another expected point of entry for my buck. As I turned slightly to the right to reposition my aim, something appeared in the corner of my right eye. I didn't have time to deal with this intrusion. This annoying thing in my peripheral vision would just have to wait…I was busy right now waiting on what was sure to be a trophy buck—the big one, my badge of honor.

Seconds seemed like minutes as I waited for the deer to come busting out of the woods. Heart pounding, teeth clenched, breathing irregular, but this thing to my right…this absolutely annoying thing was trying to distract me from doing what I had so wisely and intelligently come here to do. Several moments passed and as much as I hated to admit, it sounded as if the dogs were going further away from me. A brief moment of calm triggered my remembrance of something moving to my immediate right. As I stood, I looked to my right to cuss whatever was there, and when I did I faced the absolute shock of my hunting life! All I could see were horns!

The big oak I was sitting beside had protected me from being seen by the enormous creature standing uncharacteristically still on the opposite side of the tree. Unbelievably, I was face to face with the King of the Woods—Mr. Big Bucka himself! Only the sight of him within five feet of my face scared the total deer-killing, big wise hunter, badge-seeking ability right out of me! Startled beyond words at the sight and unexpected proximity of this huge buck, I literally threw my gun down in shock or fear, I'm still not sure which, and ran (I did) into the ankle deep, partially frozen pond, and fifty feet from my deer stand. I stood silently as I realized what had just happened.

Scared, embarrassed, and still excited, I turned back toward the oak that had only moments before been the site of the hunted hunter. Maybe I could recover from my fright, find my gun, and kill this monster, but as the cold water began seeping into my boots, reminding me of the cold, another frigid reality set in—he was gone forever! I remember thinking, *That old buck is somewhere laughing his horns off telling his buddies about the great hunter who found what he was looking for.*

Even a fourteen-year-old, south Georgia hunter doesn't tell this story until he is an old man.

10) The Sword

My grandfather attended Gordon Military College in the late 1920s, and as with all attendees, he received a beautiful ceremonial sword that became a family heirloom. Richard B. Russell Jr. was a roommate, and for years his letters, after becoming Governor and later a US Senator, were cherished memorabilia from that era, the 1930s. The sword, uniform, and letters are kept together.

The family connection to the Russell family would surface again many years later on St. Catherine's Island—another story for another time. This story, however, is about a sword, a family heirloom that digressed from a revered piece of family history to toy for child's play. Our plan for years was to pry the sword away from Glynn County, bringing it home to Liberty where it could lead charges into battle, kill imaginary enemies, and ceremoniously knight those in the neighborhood who earned such high honor.

Though in its scabbard, it dragged on the ground when strapped around our waste. Repeatedly my poor grandfather would tell us, "It is for ceremonies only; it's not a battle sword." These words meant little to us because of all the toy swords put in our toy chest, none compared to this beauty—a real sword!

Through the years, the sword took a predictable beating. We'd outgrown our childish play, so something new had to be devised for its use. Practical jokes were a big part of our teenage life, and one day an idea hatched! Perhaps yet the sword would fulfill its greatest mission—scare the bejesus out of some friends, creating a great story to be told over and over for years. In order for this idea to have maximum effect, we needed some of our unsuspecting Richmond Hill friends to come for a night visit. Our close friends knew us well and were always on guard for pranks.

Maxwellton on Colonel's Island held a certain mystique. It was always posted as private, a relatively large land mass containing very few homes, and none lived in on a permanent basis. Stories often emerged about Maxwellton—its wildlife, big cats, dog killing hogs, albino and solid black deer, bobcats, monstrous rattlesnakes, and ghost stories that emerged from the big house from multiple parties who stayed there.

Strange screams in the night that would make the hair on your neck stand straight up, and a big cat with paw and claw marks revealing his large size. Some speculated he escaped a circus roaming these parts for food. Several cows were killed—domesticated animals now, would humans be next as the old cat aged? A shark attack years earlier cost a man his leg, and later his life. The Coast was the perfect setting for our next caper.

Scary things happened at Maxwellton, and most of our friends were aware of the mystery surrounding the area. For this reason, it was easy to pile one more mystery to the list—the sword.

With great preparation, we began to tell our friends about a mysterious sword appearing in the woods at night—a flaming sword out of nowhere, perhaps the result of a curse placed against anyone who comes here. Thus far, no one had been hurt or killed, but with each sighting, the sword came closer to humans and to our house. Was it trying to tell us something, or was this the ultimate warning, driving us inside the only inhabited house on this side of the island? The rumor was spread over several weeks to legitimize our story.

The setting for this prank was set. Our home on the island had been an old oyster processing plant with very high ceilings, thirty feet or more. My granddaddy covered the walls, ceilings, and floors with heart pine. The great room sat under these high ceilings, with a featured fireplace built from ballast rock unloaded by English ships and gathered in the Riceboro River by my daddy. This great room was further adorned by a magnificent ship's wheel from a sunken sailing vessel off the north end of St. Catherine's Island, a gift to my grandfather from the late Edward J. Noble who owned St. Catherine's Island.

Ornate features had strategic prominence in this open setting. Above the beautiful ballast rock fireplace was a shined and shaped mantle from which a shofar hung and ancient wall clock stood. Placed on either end of this mantle were two ship's lanterns from the same St. Catherine's shipwreck. Furniture was mostly wood from cypress trees felled and milled on the island.

The fireplace was the centerpiece for the magnificent room, with a large round coffee table that centered the room. The table was used for meals not taken at the main dining table, drinks, magazines, and of course, card games. What teenage boy in the 60s didn't like to play poker?

High above the poker table was a missing pine knot that left a perfect hole in the high up ceiling. I actually saw a little rat poke his head out of that knot one night and survey the room below. So, by now you must be wondering what a pine knot hole in a high scary house has to do with some Richmond Hill teenagers who've been drilled for two or three weeks about a cursed sword that appears out of nowhere, and surely is about kill somebody.

Fishing line was abundant at Maxwellton. We tied the hard-to-see line to an unseen sword handle hanging from the thirty-foot ceiling with the sword blade pointing straight down. By climbing into the attic, we were able to drop the line through the knot hole, tie off the sword handle, and raise our sword to the high ceiling. With a few practices we developed the perfect drop into center table—a perfect stick every time. Dong!

With practice now complete, it was time to have poker night at Maxwellton with some of our unsuspecting Richmond Hill friends. Of course they were greeted with tales of recent sword sightings very near the house. Demonstratively (to give life to the prank), we ourselves were so frightened that shotguns were placed in the house for protection. We were careful to let them know that though the sword had never come in the house, we were prepared if it did!

The secret fish line that connected the sword's release from the ceiling was controlled the ultimate co-prankster, Richard D. (Ricky) Dykes. I was to tap Ricky's foot when the line was to be released, creating the perfect drop and stick for maximum effect. Perfect timing was after the cards had been dealt with cards in hand, not out in the middle of the table, but first, we must stir up more fear about the sword.

Just as sword fever was generating more interest than poker, the tap came and the cursed sword came flying, almost unseen as all had been told, now sticking with a thud in the middle of the table! Shock! Then, fright! Then, flight as four boys from the Hill met in the same doorway at the same time—screaming, hollering, pushing, shoving to get out! Before we could regain our composure and let these lads know they had been pranked, their truck cranked and sped down Maxwellton Road. We had to fly to catch them before Midway, but we did, finally convincing them, through our laughter, that this was all a prank and to return to the scene of the crime.

We relived each moment with them, except this time, they too found great humor in their own actions. We laughed that night for hours reliving moment by moment and small details of their escape and subsequent conversations while speeding away from Maxwellton.

I think we all laughed hard rehashing the story until the sun came up, and then this one request: "We have two friends we want to bring to the next card game; can we do it again?" On multiple occasions this prank was replayed, always with the same predictable results. Life-long friends and new acquaintances alike were easy prey to this heart-stopping prank with a guarantee of lifetime laughter. Even years after, when running into one of these victims, we laughed!

The stunt was pulled six or seven times until my daddy noticed multiple sword tip holes in his coffee table. Then, it stopped!

11) Two Warriors

Hog hunting hit South Georgia with a vengeance in the early to mid 60s as the feral hog population exploded. Wild boars brought top dollar if caught and delivered (alive) to the many professional hunting preserves popping up all over Tennessee and North Carolina. In those days, youngsters never tired of hunting, and here was a sport in which no restrictions existed on how or when we could hunt, and we were getting paid! So as not to interfere with the preferred deer hunting of fall and early winter, these hunts were scheduled in winter, spring, and summer, and our property, Maxwellton Plantation on Colonel's Island, was the perfect setting.

Catching wild hogs is a bit more dangerous than simply shooting them, as boars, particularly big ones, have a nasty disposition toward dogs, people, and being caught. First, you must locate a track or trail, and this can prove difficult unless you have dogs specifically trained for such a task. Often trails took us deep in the woods to find these skittish animals, which meant the quarry had to be tied and hauled for miles to get back to the truck and cage.

Big boars usually have big tusks, all the more to cut you or the dogs trained to bay and eventually catch the hog. Preferred boar sizes could range from 300 to 500 pounds. We were paid by the pound, so the bigger, the better. Our family land and friends with trained dogs meant that we never lacked components for a planned hunt or spontaneous outing.

One particular old boar had stumped us for well over a year, and nobody seemed to have dogs to catch this large, agile, and very fast hog. From what

we could tell, he was the biggest boar on the property with one strange char-
acteristic—his tusks were unusually small. His speed and quickness more than
made up for any shortcoming he may have lacked with small tusks, as he would
run with great speed away from trailing dogs, and finally when bayed, stand
and fight like no wild boar we had dealt with. His lightning quick reflexes
would send dogs flying in all directions, and no catch dog could get close
enough to get a grip on him. I had a healthy respect for this fighter, as I had
seen him bayed enough to know his determination and fierce fighting ability.
If I didn't know better, I might think he enjoyed it! Honestly, I respected him.

As this bruiser's reputation grew, so did interest from hog hunters around
coastal Georgia. Every pack of dogs that arrived to catch this bad boy went
away with broken and cut dogs, some (dogs) even losing their life in the quest.
This tusk-less beast met no dog he could not conquer, which raised hackles
on the backs of dog owners. As it became more evident that no one had a so-
lution, talk of killing him surfaced. I was dead against it! He was of no value
dead—his meat worthless; besides, he offered a challenge that no hog man had
met, and as long as he lived, there would always be some hunter to step up—
his legend would grow!

The last time I saw him alive, we had him bayed in a large palmetto patch
just off a dirt road. We heard the dogs hot on him from our vantage point
on the road and charged in to see if this would be the day we finally took
him down.

The way it works, trail dogs trail him, and soon bay dogs are turned loose
to run the hog down and hopefully force him to make a stand, hence the term
"bay dogs." Once he is bayed, it is then time to move in with the catch dog
whose job it is to actually catch the hog and hold him long enough for human
hands to grasp the hog's back legs, and ultimately tie the hog off. Here is where
danger and human challenge meet. If the catch dog loses his grip, the dangerous hog can swing around and disembowel a human in seconds, as the hunter
is on his knees or prostrate with both hands on the hog's hind legs. If one leg
slips out of the hunter's hands, the hog is also free to move directly onto the
hunter, at which time other hunters must shoot or dive into the fray. A split-
second decision, either way, can have serious consequences.

As we crept closer to the scene, we began to see blood stains on the green
palmettos—a sign of the massive fight—and soon we heard shrill sounds of

ear-piercing yelps and barking from the intensely riled and injured canines. This hog was making another stand against a large pack of bay and catch dogs—they were attacking him from every angle. We could get glimpses of the fight from across the tops of the palmettos, but we were not able to get close as the hog remained uncaught. As the fight moved farther down the trail, we followed with enough distance to avoid being attacked ourselves. Dogs were now lying near the scene unable to continue, as some still fought despite being savagely cut by razor sharp teeth. This incredible warrior fought on until there remained no resistance from the dogs. Yet again, another defeated pack.

The three of us standing there realized that our fourth man, the gunman, was not yet on the scene, and almost in that same instant, the hog turned, charging the nearest human to him. Ricky Dykes, who was known for sub-human feats when facing great fear, partially wrapped his arms, as best he could, around a very large pine and shimmied up the tree, making an impossible climb, now clinging high enough off the ground to avoid being attacked. To this day I have no idea how he climbed or hung on to a pine he couldn't get his arms around. I found a little flimsy tree nearby as did our buddy, Peyton Way. The hog had all three of us treed like chased raccoons. He stood there for the longest time as if to say, "I dare one of you to come out of the tree." He literally looked up at us and stared! Within minutes, which seemed like forever, Larry Rozier came running in with the gun. Larry wanted to shoot the hog but didn't because I said, "No!" He did fire a round into the air, and the big one ambled away in no big hurry. I remember thinking he may be waiting in the edge of the palmettos to attack us when we climbed down, but he didn't.

I suspect some angry dog owners later came onto the scene and killed the tusk-less hog in vengeance for killing their dogs, leaving him lying where they killed him, and ending his tenure as king of the hill. Before this saga ended, however, another adventure loomed in the very near future.

As the tales of this hog grew, so did interest in hog hunting, as now friends who never hunted wanted in on the action. One of my early childhood heroes had been a high school athlete, Rembert Rollison, whose penchant for anything macho and outdoors impressed me. He had a reputation for his attraction to all things military, as now he was in college at a military school, and I was still a pup in middle school. He was a real gung-ho guy who later lived up to his reputation in the Republic of Viet Nam. A decorated war veteran who survived and fought for days, staving off a far superior force of well-trained North Vietnamese Regulars at Firebase Ripcord, the last big battle in the Vietnam War. Though now deceased, his actions and bravery are well documented in military history. Google Rembert Gary Rollison, Lt. Colonel US Army, and see for yourself—Rembert was no ordinary man!

Home from military school, Rembert wanted some action, and tales of an invincible hog excited him to no end. Anxious to impress, I had but a day to pull a hunt together, which is short notice for an organized effort to catch a hog. Tried as I might, I couldn't find a pack of dogs. My only hope was one man who had one very tough bulldog just might be up to the task. While the idea of a single catch dog excited Rembert, I knew without trail or bay dogs, we would literally have to be right on top of a hog for this to work. As the day began, I was not optimistic, and as that very day ended, I was lower than whale manure in a deep ocean crevice. The events of this day would remain with me for a long time, as my delinquent behavior is once again revealed in yet another story. I am not proud of the course I followed, but it happened, and the ending is too incredible not to tell.

We loaded an old truck with a borrowed bulldog who was more a family pet than a bona fide catch dog, but because the owner was a close family friend of my dad's, he reluctantly agreed when I asked to take his dog hunting. His reluctance was emphasized by his constant reminders of being careful with Butch, as he was more than a mere pet to the family. He then gave me specific instructions about feeding and watering Butch when we returned from hunting as the family was leaving town for a few days and Butch would need to be cared for. The family lived in town, so Butch was normally chained to an iron post in the back yard. Though chained, the family fed and watered him under the shade of a big oak behind their home.

Anxious to impress my hero, I soft peddled the fact that we were not there to kill a hog but to catch one. Lacking any experience or skill at this type hunting, Rembert insisted on taking his .22 rifle. I knew our chances were slim of actually happening upon a wild hog, so I thought there was little chance of Butch getting hurt, which relieved me. As soon as we reached Colonel's Island, thirty miles from town, Rembert was raring to go, bouncing out of the truck and into a thick stand of palmettos right off the road. Butch jumped out of the truck, following Rembert, and before we were even settled good, we saw Rembert leap high into the air and shoot straight down. I honestly thought he had gotten on a big rattlesnake.

Startled, I called, "Did you get him?"

He answered, "Yes."

"What is it; what is it, Rembert?"

His answer froze me. "Butch!" he said.

"What? Where did you shoot him, Rembert?"

His second answer froze me even more: "Right between the eyes!"

I was sick. How on God's green earth would I ever explain this? I leaped from the truck bed and over the palmettos to see if my worst nightmare had come true. It had! Rembert had made a clean shot, apparently startled by the dog, shooting him squarely between the eyes. I wanted to freaking cry as I saw Butch lying there with a tiny squirt of blood oozing from his head. I picked Butch's lifeless body up and carried him back to the truck. My hero was now a goat, and he knew it. His trigger-happy, gung-ho crap had created big problems for me. The hunt was obviously over as I racked my brain as to how I would ever explain this. We rode around the island and talked about burying Butch, but I couldn't get a handle on doing anything but taking him home. And that's what we did. We took him right back to his chain, chained him to his collar, leaving water and food behind. It would be two days before the family returned, and other than wiping the little bit of oozing blood, he looked like he was sleeping rather than seeing all his buddies in dog heaven.

I rode by the next day, and he was still lying in the same position—I didn't stop. The family would be home the next day, and the inevitable call would come. I would decide whether to deny any knowledge of his death or come clean—I would know the right answer when I faced the question. I waited and tortuously waited for the next day. I slept little, tossing and turning over how to deal with this nightmare. I didn't know what time the family would be home, but all day, I waited for what was surely coming. As morning turned to afternoon, no call; as afternoon turned to night, no call. I knew they had to be home. Perhaps they assumed he died of natural causes and never attached his death to the hunt. Tomorrow would surely tell.

Nothing. No call, no news, no anything from my dad or the owner. What was going on? Puzzled, I rode by the house again to see anything that would answer my now bedazzled mind. Nothing prepared me for what I was about to see, and I mean absolutely nothing! To my shock, and to my greatest amazement, Butch was sitting up in his normal spot in the backyard, looking as normal and healthy as he did the day we picked him up. I was clueless as to how this could be, yet in that instant, I didn't care. Though I didn't do this, I wanted to jump out of the vehicle, run across that yard, and joyously lick Butch like dogs do when they haven't seen their owner in a while. I was so stunned and happy I couldn't hold my emotions. I think I cried tears of pure joy. I now realized why there was no call. Butch was fine, but how? The answer to this mystery would not unravel for several more years, but obviously, Rembert's bullet had not killed Butch.

As fate would have it, Butch's owner later moved to our property on Colonel's Island, and Butch spent his old age happily enjoying the freedom to run about and not be staked to a post. He died at an old age and was buried on our property. I always intended to dig him up after the family moved. Several years later they moved, and I dug. I only wanted to see one part of old Butch, and that was his skull. And just as I suspected, a hole was there, right between the two eye sockets. Obviously the small .22 bullet penetrated without dealing the thick-skulled bulldog a fatal blow. The bullet had knocked him out, which we mistook for sure death.

I honestly cannot answer what I would have said if the inevitable call had come, but I'm damn happy we didn't bury old Butch!

12) The Fortune Teller – Summer 1964

In the 1960s, a typical weekend night in rural Hinesville consisted of riding the roads on the coast, going to the drive-in, or hanging out at a local eatery. The search for something new was always the challenge. A fortune teller had opened in a house out on the edge of town, and perhaps a visit to this new business would be the night's entertainment. To be perfectly honest, we were more interested in the fortune teller than having our fortune read. You see, the painted picture out front revealed a beautiful fortune telling princess waiting inside.

To add to the adventure, certain libations were sought, and in '64 that was homemade liquor. It just so happened I knew where it could be found.

Moonshine whisky can kill if it is made wrong, and delight if it is made right, or so I thought in those days. My introduction to this evil brew came about as a result of confiscated evidence (probably not the killing kind) stored in the sheriff's evidence closet in my dad's courthouse office. When too young to buy brew, you heist it from the evidence closet. With the weekend approaching and earlier successes with this method of acquiring, I encouraged myself with another attempt. The plan was to get a mason jar full, seal it tightly, and share it with the night's running buddy. Getting the stuff in a jar was not hard, as we always were looking at guns and other items taken from criminals and stored in the closet. The office staff were none the wiser as to our true reason for being there. Armed with a mason jar of shine and a new adventure to explore, we were off.

The night's first big disappointment came when we entered the house, as our beautiful princess turned into a great grandmother between the sign out front and the house inside. "Perhaps this is the greeter, and the real fortune teller is in the back," said my running buddy. In short order, we realized, as did five or six Tennessee National Guard in town for summer camp, that this was it—Granny was the princess! No new young ladies to meet tonight! The shine was warming our stomachs and offering its first kick, so between its influence and our curiosity, we opted to stay. The Guardsman left, and we were next. Her first statement was a real doozy—explaining, as she examined my palm tracing lines in my hand, "You have been drinking and occasionally engage in rowdy behavior."

Whoa! How could she know such a thing? Really brilliant, I thought. It doesn't take a rocket scientist to know that. Then, she grabbed my buddy's hand and told him the same thing—we weren't impressed! She finished him, ending by telling him he would divorce his first wife. She then turned all of her powers on me, acting as if she was going into some kind of trance. She made a trembling motion with her head as if receiving some supernatural revelation. She told me her powers worked better on me than my friend, and the way she was contorting her face and mumbling, I kind of believed her.

She paused for a while before saying that she now had a clear view of my future. She proceeded by stating that the next three Fridays in a row, I would come face-to-face with death. She said I would live a charmed life and dodge death many times in later years.

Big deal, I thought as we left the house, laughing at ourselves for wasting five dollars on a painted sign. I thought no more of this visit than I would any other non-event in life, so when the following Friday rolled around, the thought of dying never entered my mind.

THE FIRST FRIDAY:

It was a hot summer day and time for a little skiing in the Half Moon River. Olin Fraser, my lifelong friend, and I took his daddy's newly repaired boat (a small seventeen footer) out into open water. Olin would start out on his slalom, ski until he was tired, and then it would be my turn. As was the norm, I sat on the boat's outside edge, feet in the seat while steering so as to keep an eye on the front of the boat, the steering wheel, and Olin at the rear. This visual advantage far exceeded any perceived danger of driving a boat while dangerously sitting on its outside edge. We had done it many times with never an issue. However, for some reason on this day, Olin's sharp cut of the ski turned the boat dramatically and out I flew...backwards! I landed so close to the boat that the engine's propellers passed near my side and the outside edge of the boat missed my head by inches.

Olin saw it all from his vantage point on the ski, skiing to me and letting go of the rope. There we were bobbing in the Half Moon River together, watching the newly repaired boat go flying down the channel with no driver. The boat began to make a slight arc, and instead of continuing straight away from us, it turned and headed back around toward the marina, the Half Moon Marina, full of boats and people!

Something comical happened at this point: one that we witnessed, the other we were told. A visiting family from a nearby farm was fishing on one of several floating docks at the marina. Some were none swimmers. Upon seeing a boat skipping across the river with no driver or passenger, ski rope bouncing wildly behind it, the family panicked, all converging on the single lane ramp at once. They were scrambling to get off the dock and out of the way of the unattended missile heading their way, and the one way out created a scene that landed several in the water. We found humor when there was little to be found!

Fortunately, the boat turned again, missing the dock entirely, exposing the family melee taking place on the dock. It was during this aspect of the event, which was now catching the attention of many onlookers from land, that a classic coastal phrase was born and repeated many times: "Captem Allen, Captem Allen, little Olin boat goin don de ribber...ain't nobidy in em!" Allen Branch, the marina owner, told this story many times over the years referencing his helper, William Anderson, a Geechee net maker whose steep brogue and warm charm made him one of the most beloved men of color on the coast. I loved hearing him talk, and years later, I did a Public Television documentary that featured William and other children and grandchildren of slaves.

The boat made several other turns and ultimately headed for a steep bank and up in the air, flying into the Autry family's yard. I remember hearing the sickening sound of the props trying to turn in dirt, as the motor died a slow agonizing death —but hey, it was Friday number one, and I was still alive!

THE SECOND FRIDAY:

Friday number two was approached with a little more caution as the irony of the previous Friday was, in my opinion, purely coincidental...but cautious optimism was my play! A nice day of sailing was planned as Olin's dad purchased a used but nice sailing vessel from his family on Hilton Head. The boat was equipped with radios, compasses, and other electronics that we saw little of in this part of the country. The big radio was most impressive with great sound from our favorite AM Station, Big Ape Radio out of Jacksonville, Florida.

On this particular trip, Olin's sister, Claire, was onboard along with longtime friends, Angie Clark and her Savannah cousin, Ann Yeomans. A little sailing in the river posed no threat, and this calm day would prove that Granny's fortune telling was a fluke, or so I reasoned. I thought little of the fact that extra beer was loaded for the cruise, as the day's heat warranted cold beverages. I loved hanging out with this crowd—laughter seemed to be spontaneous when we got together.

The July heat placed demand on the cool beverages as boredom was setting in with river sailing. Olin's dad had forbidden us to go seaward, but he wouldn't be home for a while. The next thing I knew we were headed out the North Newport River toward St. Catherine's Island. Life was great. A gentle breeze turned into ocean wind, and boredom gave way to excitement, now accentuated by a strong beer buzz. We were seaward!

Adults have reasons for telling teenagers not to do something, but teenagers are the most intelligent people on earth—always have been, always will be! With the wind in our sails, beer in our belly, we were indestructible, invincible, and enjoying life—great music, great friends, and out on the water. What else could we want? Certainly not one of those fast-moving summer storms that can pop up over an island and catch you entirely unprepared. No, we didn't want or expect that. Storms coming in from the east and ocean side of the island often have high wind and lightening that come suddenly and violently. And yes, this good time sailing venture was about to turn nasty.

The first sign of real trouble was the ominous black clouds rolling over St. Catherine's, soon followed by wind that caught our outstretched sails, yanking the boat sideways. There was a reason we were told to stay safely in the protection of the harbor. We didn't know how to sail! We could hardly maneuver in a gentle breeze, yet now we faced gusting winds, rocky seas, and in short order, lightning and torrential rain. Don't know if you have ever been on the open water in a lightning storm, but if you haven't, you'll ask Jesus into your heart quickly! It is terrifying!

Olin and I tried desperately to turn the boat around as we were at the tip of the North Newport in the open water of the Intracoastal Waterway. The wind snatched the boat violently from side to side as lightning struck nearby, possibly in the marsh. The girls realized we were in trouble but bravely held on. In an instant, a passing fisherman, high tailing it to the hill, saw our plight and pulled alongside. There was enough room for the girls to get out. I've always been thankful to Bobby O'Neal, who risked his own safety to get the girls out of a dangerous situation. Bobby assured us that someone would be back as soon as the storm broke. Seeing the boat fade in the distance temporarily took my mind off the real issue—survive and save the boat! The wind was getting stronger and lightning strikes more frequent and close. Of the perils at hand, the frequency of lightning and its proximity scared us most. We felt hopelessly exposed. Lives are lost to lightning every year, and the Georgia coast has seen its share of these tragedies.

By now, Olin and I were hanging on with no way to take the sail down or maneuver in the storm. The boat was turning almost sideways with the high winds causing us to realize we could capsize. Strangely, the radio, now protected under the front of the boat, was still playing. With rain pouring, loud thunder and nearby lightning, the noise capturing my attention was the roar of the shifting wind on the banging sails—it was deafening! And then, as if by some fluke, the clanging stopped in eerie silence as the sail filled with wind and we made a slow-motion roll as the boat capsized. As God be my witness, the radio was playing "Cast Your Fate to the Wind" as it sank from sight, never to be heard or seen again. All the fancy gear gone, we found ourselves treading water next to the capsized sailboat.

Another Friday and another destroyed boat belonging to Olin Fraser Sr. I felt horrible. I knew how much Mr. Fraser had sacrificed to have two nice boats for his family for the summer, and now I had been part of destroying them both. We soon found an air pocket under the capsized boat, and it seemed the safest place to be. We were out of the storm and at least able to get our wits about us. Our thoughts immediately turned to the boat—we could ride the storm out and somehow get the boat turned right side up.

We soon realized this would prove to be much more difficult than anticipated. The tall mast had lodged in the mud fifteen or more feet beneath us. It was impossible to think about moving the boat unless it could be freed. While waiting for rescuers, we had nothing better to do than dive down and attempt to manually lift the mast in hope of freeing it from the mud. I went first, taking a deep breath and diving straight down in the murky water with practically zero visibility. I felt my way around the bottom, and to my surprise, sensed we could move it a little. I struggled to free it, but I realized I was running out of air fast. I bolted to the surface, and panic hit me as I realized my ankle was entangled in the rigging. Panic in critical situations is often the difference in life and death, and I was moving fast toward death with fright in full control. Suddenly, without a known reason why, calm visited me, and I was able to stop fighting to swim upward against the vice grip of the rigging. Calmly, I bent down with my arms and unwrapped the rigging and swam to the surface, even remaining calm in telling Olin I had just come close to drowning.

Another eventful Friday of destroyed boats and near death experiences, another day starting so well yet ending in heartbreak. Thousands of dollars in destruction mostly due to youthful carelessness and willful disobedience.

THE THIRD FRIDAY:

It dawned on me after escaping yet another close call that the third Friday was but a week away. I would avoid any and everything remotely dangerous, stay near my daddy, and keep away from anything that looked suspicious. I was happy to learn the following week that he wanted me to work with him on our coastal farm, Maxwellton Plantation on Colonel's Island.

When Friday came, he decided to string a barbed wire fence along the Yellow Bluff Road, which would prevent our cows from getting into anyone's yard or on the highway. Our work crew consisted of my daddy's friend, Thereon Rogers, and family farmhand, Uncle Dan "Elijah" Golfin, who at eighty or so could still work with the best of them. Many of my favorite Geechee stories came from Uncle Dan, who lived across Highway 38 from Mary Jane Yates's store, not far from our home on Colonel's Island.

The plan was for Uncle Dan and I to string the fence from post to post, while Thereon and Daddy tacked and braced the wire to the post. How was there any danger in this? None I could see. Barbed wire is strung, and our job was to hold a metal bar that the wire was wrapped around, and then simply walk. With Uncle Dan on one side and me on the other, we would string from post to post, while the other team members stretched the wire and tacked it to the post—simple enough!

As the morning passed, we made good progress, and after a quick sardine lunch at Yellow Bluff Fish Camp, we were back at it. By midafternoon, I was sure "Granny" was nothing more than mere coincidence as we worked our way toward the final stretch of road, which contained an ever so slight curve. I stayed barefooted in summer, seldom putting on shoes despite my daddy's disapproval, especially while working, but teenage intelligence often ruled! I couldn't imagine how uncomfortable those old rubber boots were that Dan always wore, yet he trudged through the hottest days of summer with those old things on his feet. I remember how liberated I thought I was to be free of boots in summer.

Just as our work entered the curve and final home stretch, the oaks that lined either side of the narrow dirt road began to sway. Generally, this is an indication of the afternoon southeast wind that cools the coast in summer, but occasionally, it can mean a coming storm. When away from the shore and surrounded by high trees, there is no real way to differentiate unless you hear approaching thunder in the distance. No thunder let me know that a great afternoon breeze was coming to cool things off; when, in fact, the day would end in great discomfort.

As I focused on getting the wire to the next post, I heard an alarming and unexpected crack of lightening behind me. I turned just in time to see a fireball running down the wire we had already strung, and before I could react, it hit the metal wire and rod we were holding. Dan's rubber boots perhaps made a difference because the lighting sent me flying, but he stood still. I remember feeling like I had been hit by a big truck as my body flew ten or twelve feet from where I was standing. I remember the sensation of flying through the air, but I do not remember hitting the ground.

My next conscience thought was waking to my daddy asking how I felt, but now instead of being on a dirt road, I was in our home on the front porch.

63

How had I gotten here? I was confused about what happened, and I kept asking how I got to the house. My body tingled, and nerves twitched uncontrollably in my body. After some time sitting there, I realized they didn't know the extent of my disorientation. I was apparently acting normal but feeling any way but...

Within a few hours, it all came back to me—the swaying trees, the curve in the road, the lighting crack and fireball. Dang, I had been struck by lightning! Apparently it hit a tree or something near enough to the metal to travel the wire, the metal bar, and ultimately, me. I flew like a flat river rock skipping over a pond! I don't know exactly how close I came to really dying during these three unusual Friday experiences, but I can tell you this: When that third Friday was over, so were my fortune telling days.

13) Troy Winn

He called me "Sporty Boy," and Stevie "Stebie." His daughter was Kathy, but to him "Cassie." To the day he died, my daddy called her "Cassie" too; he thought that was her name. His last name was Winn, but one night the State Patrol nabbed him, and he changed it to "Sikes." That story made the rounds, and he was kidded about it for years.

When I was born, Troy was there. When I first developed memory, Troy was there. He was among my first ever memories. Every Christmas Troy was there. Every deer hunt, including my first, Troy was there. Trips to the coast, squirrel hunts, mullet jumping, bailing hay, cutting wood, building anything, caring for cows and goats, Troy was there. When we forgot to feed the horse, Troy was there. When "Son" Futch's cows got into our garden, Troy was there. Gathering eggs or killing a chicken from the coup, Troy was there. When a wild hog charged me at "the flowing well," Troy was there.

He drove my high-sheriff granddaddy, cleaned anything we killed or caught, built fences, set pumps, pulled cows out of the marsh, bailed hay, fed cows, delivered TVs, refrigerators, and anything the family hardware store sold. He scalded hogs, cured hams, picked vegetables, cleaned a million deer, squirrels, coons, and fish in the process. He was Daddy's best friend. No, more a brother than friend. He didn't work for our family; he was our family. In later years when Daddy fell ill, he drove him daily, making his rounds over the county, including a daily trek to Maxwellton on Colonel's Island. They both drank Town Club, a cheap blended whisky they always purchased at Earl Dean's in Midway—sharing their little half pint bottle every workday for years.

How did this man occupy such a place in Daddy's life? I never really questioned it, but did notice as I grew older, bonds like this were not common. Many black men worked for white families, but none I knew had an actual role in the family. I remember resenting Troy's authority over me, but I accepted it as "the way it was." How had this man become so entrenched in the Sikes family? How was a bond like this even possible during a time it was impossible? These two men shared the entirety of their lives—as different as black and white, but the same in so many ways!

As the story goes, Troy was one of many children being raised by a single parent mother in the depression-ridden 1920s and 30s. His mother simply could not feed them all, so my granddaddy took a very young Troy in, building a little house behind his own near his sizable yard on the edge of town. Troy was approximately twelve and Daddy seven when Troy came to live with the family. They grew up together, getting into the normal mischief kids do, often running afoul of my granddaddy. They once climbed trees in my grandparents' yard, firing slingshot rocks at passing trucks. My granddaddy was called about this misbehavior, approached their tree with his belt drawn. Daddy climbed down and took his spanking. Troy remained in the tree all night, which I'm told sufficed for a spanking. Many stories of their childhood explained their uncanny relationship—they grew up together in a family doing all the things families do. Troy tended to the yard and many other chores on family lands and business while Daddy attended school, including college and a tour in the Navy.

I often heard of reunions when Daddy came home, deep into Hack's Pasture to check out a new hunting spot that Troy had found. They would talk of boyhood ventures and the many times Troy saved Daddy from my granddaddy's wrath. I don't think these two ever saw color when they saw each other. They both liked boxing as my granddaddy's big RCA radio broadcasted the big fights of that era—Joe Lewis and Max Schmellning, undefeated Rocky Marciano, Archie Moore, Sugar Ray Robinson, kept them glued to their chair. Later in life, I was honored to buy Pay-For-View fights they could watch together, always buying them a big bottle of Town Club to share. Troy loved Evander Holyfield and was angered beyond words when Tyson bit his ear off.

Troy shared the best and worst of times with us, and the hardest day of my young life was about to happen. The dynamic of the Sikes family changed as did Troy's role in our family.

I was eleven when my granddaddy died unexpectedly of a heart attack. We were staying with my grandparents the weekend of my grandfather's unexpected death. My parents were away, the guest of Charles Fraser on Hilton Head, who was just opening the William Hilton Inn on Sea Pines. My grandparents had a designated telephone room in their home where private calls could be made or taken, often needed for sheriff's office business. I happened to be sitting with my grandmother when the call came in about my grandfather. She was called by a distant cousin who ran her motel on Hwy 17 in Midway, ironically a short distance from where my grandfather died (near the old Midway Church). Death was not familiar to me, so hearing her say, "Are you sure, are you sure, are you sure?" was strange and scary, then tragically sad. Upon putting the phone down, I asked her what was wrong. She only answered, "I have to call Flo," my aunt who lived next door. I'd never seen her cry, yet tears were dripping in rhythmic fashion. Little did I know, but I was about to experience death for the first time, up close and personal.

Locating my dad on Hilton Head took time, but immediately family gathered as did close friends. I remember walking through my grandmother's big house, wondering what would come next. I was in a daze. I felt guilty for not "going to ride" with my granddaddy that Saturday morning. I was mad because he had blistered me the day before with a "buggy switch" picked from a bush. The house was a maze of confusion: people everywhere, some crying uncontrollably...much to take in for a small boy. I came downstairs and wandered in the kitchen, and there outside on the back steps sat Troy. I felt comfortable sitting by him, just as if he was my daddy. I'd just lost my granddaddy, who was like a daddy. My real daddy was on a faraway island, but I'd found the next best thing, Troy!

In spite of his own pain, he comforted me. He then said words that rang with prophetic truth: "A lot gone be on yo daddy shoulders!" The next days were a whirlwind. In those days, the body of the deceased was brought home and people visited, brought food, and shared memories. In the confusion of it all, I'd find that spot on the back steps again and again. For the first time in my young life, I felt some comfort being near Troy. Black folks came, always to that back door, but were welcomed warmly by my grandmother—many were close friends, which was a bit unusual for August of 1959. Troy acted as the unofficial doorman, welcoming my grandfather's many black friends.

As with all who go through that first big shock of death, my world was rocked! I was the apple of my granddaddy's eye, his first-born grandchild, a boy, born on his birthday. Though he disciplined me often, I knew he loved me, often doing things I couldn't believe. As a small boy, I wanted a boat, so to Maxwellton we went, and there sat my little boat, though bound to the yard. I rowed and rowed; later a pony and the "Legend of Star" began, the neighborhood horse who every kid in town rode. Dealing with such loss was not easy. Paul had been more father than grandfather to me. To this day, I recall cold nights he would invite us into his bedroom where a warm fire burned—we talked. I loved this. He made me feel close, so close I called him Dada, while addressing Daddy as Bobby.

Troy and Daddy bonded closer during this period as suddenly all the business and political responsibility were resting on the young shoulders of thirty-one-year-old R.V. (Bobby) Sikes. Paul Sikes was a strong personality who pretty much did things his way; Daddy had not seen the need to be the front of the spear, as his daddy filled that role, but now there seemed little choice as to how he must make decisions. Everyone, it seemed, had an opinion as to what my dad should do; even as a twelve-year-old, I remember the many directions he was given. I know he was confused because many he loved had completely different ideas as to new direction for his life.

During that period, he often turned to Troy. Troy's opinion mattered, and I believe it did because it came without motive, except what was best for my daddy and our family. I'm certainly not saying what others wanted was not entertained, but I do think Troy's advice in this life-altering decision was highly considered. You see, the big decision, among other things, was should he run for sheriff to fill the unexpired term of my grandfather. Clearly, my daddy had no desire to be sheriff, to be a leader, but circumstances pointed him in that direction.

A whirlwind came into our lives that seems never to have left, as soon Daddy was Liberty County's new sheriff, also bearing a myriad of other responsibilities, including running Paul Sikes & Son, a hardware and appliance store in downtown Hinesville. Again, Daddy and Troy were joined at the hip, as Troy and my Uncle Zeck did all appliance and pump installations and kept political obligations running smoothly. Hunts, fish suppers, political parties, and business trips seemed endless; head of the Booster's Club, Civic Organizations, singing in weddings, funerals, parties and celebrations—his schedule and responsibilities were heavy and took a toll on his health. Troy was there every step of the way. Quintuple by-pass surgery in his late 30s saved him from the inevitable heart attack that killed his daddy.

By 1992, my dad's twenty-eight years in the sheriff's office ended in defeat, his businesses and health suffering. Though still in his early 60s, he was tired and never regained the razor-sharp personality that endeared him to so many. By now, Troy was in his upper 60s, and too had run a good race as his health also suffered. With businesses closing and weary bodies, they still found reason to ride to the coast. Earl Dean was gone, but young Ted, his son, became a great friend. The tradition continued: Troy picked up Daddy, and to Ted Dean's they went, often stopping for a chat at the store, then to the coast to sit on the dock, ride the woods, or do a few chores.

Troy was the first to go, as we were scheduled to watch another fight at my house in just a few days. His death wasn't totally unexpected in his now declining health but caught us all by surprise. I don't remember exactly who broke the news to Daddy, but I knew, in advance, he wouldn't handle it well. I had seen him openly cry one time: his daddy's death. Now, his tears flowed again; outside his immediate family, he had lost the person he cherished most in this life—his dearest friend, his brother Troy!

They shared what few do, a bond that spanned race and socioeconomic status. Love truly triumphed as many knew far and wide, these two were inseparable—only death, and that only temporary.

Troy is buried under an oak tree right off Ft. Stewart, across the road from the C.R. Stanford farm. His grave is visible from the road as is my daddy's. I ride by them often...I cry! I miss them and the awesome bond they shared.

14) Friday Night Lights in Coastal Georgia

Sometimes we teammates call each other to remind ourselves it is Friday night again, just many years later! This night, December 3rd, 1965, is etched in our hearts, a defining moment for us all. It would change our lives in no small way, binding us throughout life, and give each of us a tiny edge, a small advantage, in attempting any task in life—the belief we could accomplish it.

Many years later, my coach would come back in my life and lift me from a pit of failure and defeat, simply telling me I was a winner...an encouragement came that allowed me to fight on at a time I saw no way out.

It's 8:55 P.M., just about halftime many years ago—December 3rd, 1965. It's freezing cold, heat blowers on the sidelines, hardly anyone is sitting, and Olvey Field is packed with its largest and noisiest crowd ever. A never achieved State Championship is on the line. I look around the huddle, Bill Stanford's jersey is almost ripped off, Hardy's arm is bleeding at the elbow, Candler wants Phil to give him the ball, Primo is covered in dirt, Ricky's mad—an opposing player is complaining about being gouged in the eye on the previous play. The stands are buzzing, yet I hear my own dad's laughter from his usual spot on the sidelines. How do I hear his voice so clearly? Always a mystery my whole high school career. The game is close. Our hearts are beating out of our chest—this just might be the year we do it! A State Football Championship! The whole county wants it as much as we do. Signs are everywhere, the town is decorated in blue and gold, festivities, parades, neighboring schools and players attending our practices, phone calls, newspapers, and local TV. Years were poured into this night, hours of practice, pain, and sacrifice—literally, blood, sweat, and tears for years, since the fourth grade, now seniors.

A Coach was brought to Liberty County when we were in grade school. His job: win championships. In those days, first through twelfth grade attended the same school, Bradwell Institute. All who wanted to play, starting in fourth grade, could come out for some form of organized football. We, the youngest class to start, delighted in learning to play together at nine years of age. Many on the field that Championship night were seventeen, playing together since 1957 at age nine.

We were molded, trained, and taught Coach Hokey Jackson's philosophy of life—never quit, complain, or cry, a style that would be scorned and ridiculed in this day of entirely different coaching philosophies. He pounded in us that great character makes great champions. He kept close tabs on us in the off season, occasionally punishing us for youthful mistakes. I hated and loved him at the same time! When we got hurt on the field, he would tell us, "Spit on it, and be a dog." I never really knew what that meant, but I knew it's meaning—move past the pain! There are other aspects of his toughness toward us that would make current school boards cringe. We knew he was tough as nails and rough on us, but confident that when others wilted, we would not. The ones of us still on the planet have some of that in us today. Personally, I've had to learn both the positive and negative side of that philosophy as I'm an old man now. By the way, basic training in the army was a breeze compared to Hokey Jackson summer camps.

Manchester, at the time, was the biggest and perhaps fastest high school football team we had ever seen. Bobby Dodd, legendary coach at Georgia Tech, was in the stands as were other college and high school coaches. We were later told that many college coaches didn't think we could stay on the field with such a big and fast team. We were 13 and 0 when they came blazing onto the field, and even though they looked like a small college team, we were confident we would win. We had been trained and convinced we would not lose, even to what appeared a much superior force.

Entire teams we had played during the season or in the playoffs lined the sidelines, becoming some of our loudest supporters—everybody wanted the Class B State Championship back in South Georgia. The enormous chill of the night did nothing to denigrate the warmth of extreme unity felt in southeast Georgia that night. There was a unity in our community I haven't felt before or since. Our friends from Liberty High, the black high school, and old folks who had never seen a football game were there to spur us on.

Manchester scored first, as their fleet-footed running back showed us speed we hadn't seen all year. These guys were big and fast, well-muscled, and skilled blockers and tacklers. We read their press, which seemed all true, but just as it became evident we were much outclassed, something else kicked in: our belief that we could and would win. The thought of losing really didn't cross our mind—we believed, and we won!

The scene on the field after the game was pandemonium and celebration—joy unspeakable! The locker room even more so! For that one brief moment, our community was one—no axes to grind, squabbles, or fights, and to some extent we were local heroes, young men of excellence, high achievers.

Today, our team is well into its transition into the next life—what a night we shared together! None of us knew how deeply this would affect the remainder of our lives, but we knew immediately something of great importance had happened.

Winning a high school football championship was a big deal in 1965—it is still a big deal for all who played, uniting us as brothers 'til death, giving us a little boost in life when one was needed. Bradwell 13/Manchester 9.

15) Two Men

Many influences shape us—surroundings, events, culture, experiences, but people have the greatest impact on our most positive outcomes. I was fortunate to have two men in my young impressionable life who set a standard that clearly defines me today. I am shaped by much of what I gleaned from my rich experiences with these two. I think and reason much by the standards they set for me.

Our young life is a constant search for identity, personality, and character, and these two were rich in all aspects of aspiration and inspiration. These early in life models led many young men, more by example than instruction—one intentionally, one somewhat unintentionally. The results were the same. Mentoring, intentional and otherwise, to young and old alike, is critical to society and the future of our country, as those we accept as trusted models create a resemblance (in us) that look like them. The greatest tribute to any man is his good character duplicated by those he influences.

I am thankful to my dad, Bobby Sikes, and Hokey Jackson, my coach, for values that will be with me until I breathe my last breath. I am amazed when I see these men in my own children, which I clearly do.

One of these men created boundaries of decency, a model of kindness especially to those less fortunate. His tender heart was more what he did than what he said. A friend shared a story recently from his rough childhood, a day in which his alcoholic father had beat him and sent him to a nearby field to build a dog pen in subfreezing temperatures. The field was visible from the highway. As the story goes, his physical discomfort was much less burdensome than his torn heart. Without notice, a man from the highway arrived to help and comfort him. He stayed until the last nail was driven. That man was the sheriff of the county and my daddy, who helped and offered words of encouragement that things would get better.

While one created boundaries, the other created a desire to achieve, to run a specific course with goals and objectives. His great lesson was persistence and patience—the knowledge that you are never defeated until you give up. This teaching would serve me well as failure in life would visit me often. In November of 1997, I gathered 125 employees in the back of my warehouse to tell them the banks were cutting us off and that this was their last day of work—the company was closing. I was given a short time to vacate my offices. A few days after the dreaded announcement, my wife and new baby accompanied me to clean out my desk and collect a few personal items—I had never felt so low! As I sadly looked over my old office, lost dreams, and misplaced effort, I was overwhelmed by complete failure and lack of future for my new wife and baby.

Suddenly, I heard the front door open and someone walking down the long hallway leading to my office—I recognized the sound of those footsteps. At one of the lowest points of my entire life, Coach Jackson walked in. He put his hand on my shoulder and said, "Remember this, Clay, you aren't a loser; you are a winner, and you will come back from this." His words carried me through the many years that it took to recover, but solidly, those words lifted me though one impossible situation after another.

16) My Buddy

Elijah "Dan" Golphin, the grandson of slaves, lived and died within a few hundred feet of his birthplace in eastern Liberty County. Born in an unknown year, Dan worked for our family on Maxwellton Plantation, off and on, as long as I can remember. Strong, wise, and witty, this old man, who was from another time, introduced me through his stories, to life on the coast as it once was—mules, wagons, kerosine lamps, basket weaving, crops, and "food from de ribber—scrimps, crobb, and de fishes." All told in thoroughbred Geechee.

As the years passed, my friendship with him deepened. Many times upon returning home from college, I scampered to his house before going home. I so enjoyed our visits that included hours of countless stories. Dan was known to make a little shine and share it, and yes, we sipped, right there in the back yard, sitting on Coca-Cola crates. "Jar Whisky" we called it, 'cause that's what we drank from.

Dan died in the late 70s, but before he did, I was able to convince Georgia Educational Television to do thirteen hours of crucial interviews with Dan and others, some the actual children of slaves. These interviews captured the story of coastal Georgia in the post-Civil War era. Recognizing that this part of living history was soon to vanish forever, I interviewed from the stories I had heard most of my life. Priceless!

Elijah Golphin, my buddy. Every time he would see me, he addressed me as "my buddy," not as Clay—in fact, never as Clay, but always "my buddy." I miss him terribly!

17) Lesson from a Stranger

The old man rolled his tobacco, enjoyed his smoke, and sat on the same store front bench every Saturday morning. Facing the seaside village's Main Street and nearby fishing pier, he seemed to be Hemingway's *Old Man and the Sea*.

The etched lines in his face revealed years of time, as his weather-beaten skin told its own story. His fingers were gnarled, his white hair long, touching his scruffy beard in spots. His open denim shirt revealed a darkened tan. A man of the sun. Perhaps a fisherman, a net maker, or a builder of boats, but honestly, to me, he looked a king, a man of royalty—his age served him well.

I often saw him there on his bench as I slowly jogged through the village, always wanting to stop and ask him questions. He looked like a human relic filled with wisdom, yet robust, like people living near the sea often do. I sensed he might have something to tell me, maybe something important. At the very least he could tell me about this beautiful island I now lived on.

As another Saturday rolled around, it was settled in my mind. Today, I would stop and scratch this curious itch. I would find out why this old fellow had such a grip on me. As I jogged into the village leading to the pier, I anxiously looked toward the bench where he always sat—he wasn't there!

Maybe he was inside the little shop, hadn't arrived yet, or something. I stopped, asked the storekeeper, "Where is the old man who always sits out front?"

"He left us this week," she stated in a saddened tone.

It didn't quite hit me. "Excuse me?"

Now, in a distinctly clear voice, "He passed on, son!"

I was deeply moved, almost depressed, as I left the store in shock, mumbling, "I am so sorry!" Why did I sense such loss over someone I never knew? Why did I feel this gut-aching regret? What had I missed not knowing this regal old man of the sea? I'll never know, but he taught me one of life's great lessons—the pain of regret is steeped in finality. Make decisions in life that leave the least room for regret.

18) A Sleepy Town Wakes Up
– Statesboro 1971

The long walk to school with a ton of books under my arm (long before bookbags were around) would end forever. No more long walks, no more school, and no more Statesboro. College graduation was right around the corner. Only a few short years before it all seemed impossible. Sitting in an English class my freshman year, graduation seemed a million miles away.

My long walks from downtown Statesboro to main campus at Georgia Southern had been memorable—a place of solitude and reflection. Time to think and sort through issues. Many decisions were made during this time, decisions that would affect the remainder of my life. The tug to go home to Liberty County was birthed on this walk, as constantly I dreamed. I had what I can only describe as a premonition during this time, seeing myself heavily involved in real estate in my now sleepy little town.

During the spring of 1971, things in Statesboro were buzzing—I was graduating with the first ever criminal justice class in the entire university system; offers for careers were coming. Bill Beardsley, former head of GBI, had been selected to start the new criminal justice curriculum a few years before; Georgia Southern was to be the initiator, and there I sat in the middle of it all, about to graduate. Beardsley had many connections, and his goal was to launch this new curriculum with good jobs aligned for those who graduated. Law enforcement had never been a goal, though it runs deep in my family; I was much more focused on real estate than criminal justice, but criminal justice required only one math class. Everyone assumed law enforcement coursed in my veins, but the truth rested in my math skills, or lack thereof.

With no real intention, interesting criminal justice opportunities were opening at the federal level; one seriously attracted my attention. Curiosity took me closer until my then military father-in-law offered an ultimatum: "Don't do this if you intend to stay married to my daughter." He knew the institution well and thought little of my future there. As it turned out, many years later, I didn't stay married to his daughter either, but I took this as a further sign and opted to return to my hometown.

Nothing was happening in Hinesville, Georgia in the spring of 1971; in fact, nearby Ft. Stewart, long viewed as the economic engine of Liberty County, was in virtual caretaker status with less than 3,000 associated military personnel at Stewart proper. The 1970 census for Hinesville was 6,132. Nothing to support my dream of dealing in dirt. After all, my name is Clay, and buying and selling land intrigued me.

My next obstacle was paternal. My dad played a part in bringing Interstate Paper to Liberty County and had many connections at the Mill. He had located a good paying job and insisted, at graduation, I take it. Interstate Paper Company was the biggest thing in the county at the time. However, my sacrifice in getting an education was stout—working two jobs, married with one car, and having to study hard to make grades—it was my heart to move into real estate. The Power House at the Riceboro Mill was not where I wanted to be. I wanted to buy and sell land, build houses, set up a brokerage operation, maybe even develop land, but my paternal influence saw otherwise, and this was a problem. Winning my daddy's approval had always been a driving force, much more than I realized, in pursuing my dream over his strong objection. Against his will, perhaps for the first time in life, I started my drive to my dream with a temporary job with the City of Hinesville as its first ever industrial director. Starting salary was $8,500 annually.

I knew federal funds would soon fizzle and industrial development would only be a short stop before my goal could be achieved, and by November of 1973, things were coming to an end. Finally, I was free to pursue my heart; the only problem was little to no market in the area. Very soon that would all change. In early fall of 1974, I received a call from my dad instructing me to come to the courthouse where his sheriff's office was located (ironically the same office my grandfather occupied for the twenty-plus years). I knew something was up as I heard excitement in his normally unexcitable expression, and soon I would learn why this calm man was not so calm.

As I entered the front office, the door to his office proper was closed; this normally meant no interruptions, but today, it would be okay as I was invited. Upon entering I quickly recognized two men I knew well but seldom saw in the sheriff's office: lawyer Charles Jones and the county's biggest businessman, Glenn Bryant. Shortly after my arrival, Jimmy Floyd, president of the local bank, and Mayor Carl Dykes entered. What on earth was I about to learn? These men all were recognized leaders, and all had a hand in any major development in Liberty County—I knew without question something big was happening!

I genuinely felt out of place amongst these giants, but I accepted that I was to be a part of whatever was about to unfold. Charlie spoke first and began by telling us his dear friend, Senator Sam Nunn, would soon arrive as would Congressman Howard (Bo) Ginn, and "Bo" Callaway (from Georgia), who was then Secretary of the Army. An announcement was forthcoming, and soon, Hinesville as we knew it would change dramatically, but first we would meet privately before the matter would be announced to the world.

The plan was to meet the dignitaries at Charlie's office, a few hundred yards down Court Street from the courthouse. His then small office was connected to the offices of Judge Paul Caswell (my great uncle), as he too joined us for the preliminary preview of the day's events. Again, Charlie spoke in his usual articulate manner, explaining details of just how the Pentagon, at Senator Nunn's urging with a push of Secretary Calloway, decided to activate the 24th Infantry Division, a mechanized infantry force easily deployable from nearby ports of Savannah, Charleston, Brunswick, and Jacksonville. Logistically, the vast land resource, 286,000 acres, was perfect for mechanized training, and the nearby ports made rapid deployment a natural. Ft. Stewart had fallen in the bull's eye of a permanent growth strategy by the Pentagon.

I couldn't help but think Hinesville was about to change - a sleepy town where everybody knew everybody. I remember nervously asking my dad about changes to our town, and he quickly reminded me 80,000 troops were once "housed" at Ft. Stewart during World War II. That was hard for me to imagine but so too was the temporary nature of this sprawling military complex once known as Camp Stewart. Though I am old enough to remember Camp Stewart, the bulk of my life it had a more permanent connotation as Ft. Stewart, even though there was talk of closing it at one point.

In short order, our very important guest arrived, and soon the future was explained by the bespectacled Senator. A powerful man in DC, Sam Nunn headed the Senate Arm Services Committee, overseeing millions of dollars in defense spending, and now it appeared some of that money would flow back into Liberty County. This, at the time, was welcomed relief as businesses were dying on the vine from the up and down nature of Ft. Stewart. Since the days of 80,000 temporary troops, Stewart saw decline post World War Two, an uptick during the Korean War, another decline until Vietnam, and as that war wound down, so did Ft. Stewart.

Our local economy was tied to the fortunes of the military base, and many were painfully suffering at this very moment in time. Some would later complain about growth in the area, but those complaints did not come from those who owned small businesses, those who were trying to pay bills and feed families. We were soon out the door of Charlie's office, headed to the courthouse steps where many folks were gathering: TV crews, reporters, local elected officials, and curiosity seekers. The short walk spawned more questions to Secretary Calloway—Charlie pressed him for numbers. His answer caught my ear, and I remember exactly the answer and exactly the spot on East Court Street where it was said: in front of our family-owned Standard Oil Service Station. Calloway answered with a question, "Initially or eventually, Charlie?" That was an interesting answer to me as it indicated a progressive buildup.

"8,000 will begin arriving soon, and eventually, those numbers will swell to 16,000."

To the older folks, these numbers didn't mean much when compared to 80,000, but one significant point was made by our guest: "These are permanent troops with families, all of which will be moving here."

And then, Calloway's next question froze me in my tracks. "Is this community ready for 8,000 troops, many of which have families?"

I reflected back to my long walks to school seeing myself deeply involved in real estate in my hometown. I had seen something so clearly, and now it was happening. Though I held the necessary licensing, I knew nothing about running or building a real estate business— I didn't even know how to write a VA contract, and no one else in town did either. What would I do when families came to my office? There was much to do, much to learn, and much that had to be accomplished, all of which had to be compacted into a short span of time. What to do when your dream comes true and you are unprepared?

Luckily, I connected with A.G. Wells, a local land surveyor who also had recently passed the bar and real estate brokerage exam. His considerable intelligence and skills could be matched by my drive and dream, and together, we would build Liberty County's newest business: Liberty Realty. Interestingly, Hinesville had one part-time real estate office owned and managed by P.D. Fowler, brother-in-law to well-known real estate auctioneer Brown Childs of Statesboro. Mr. Fowler had been more appraiser than broker and knew very little about the sales process either.

Mr. Wells, however, proved to be a godsend, an attorney, land surveyor, and real estate broker all rolled into one package and the only man in the state to hold all three licenses. We opened our office on East South Street, right across from City Hall and next door to Liberty Pharmacy, owned and operated by John and Sue Nutting. John, who I had met several years prior, turned out to be a mentor and friend. He was an older, more experienced businessman who took an interest in me. We often talked for hours about the business opportunity now coming our way and just how to handle it. His business counsel far exceeded mine, sowing wonderful ideas into me. Ironically, many years later, I would have the same opportunity with his son, Bill.

Just like the weatherman predicting snow in South Georgia that seldom comes, we believed new families were coming but didn't see or hear from them. Like the long-lost snow, maybe the army changed its mind. Our offices lacked customers; where were they? They were promised, but when would they arrive? Every minute of every day was busy, learning the market, learning exactly how to put together contracts, how to anticipate working with customers, and how to find available houses to sell, but still, no customers. Weeks turned into months without any real sign something big was happening. Then, one Friday morning, everything changed, and it hasn't stopped in fifty years! In one hour, seven families invaded my small lobby, all needing homes. I panicked! Finally, it was time to put all the preparation to work, to walk out what I had seen and expected long ago.

19) Life in an Army Town

The pretty young mother was doing her best, but the needs of two small children momentarily overwhelmed her. The resilient strength that had carried her since losing her soldier seemed to be waning—an unclear future and engulfing loneliness painfully settled in her heart.

I saw it etched in her face from my table in the army town cafe. She wandered in. I knew who she was; I had seen her picture and knew her story from the local news. Another brave husband had given his life. Now, left to fend for herself, another non-combatant victim of war— empty, bereft, uncertain.

My heart was broken for this young stranger, my misting eyes revealing me. Another war had made its claim on another family. What would she do? Where would she go from here? When will this end? Another young life filled with death. I weep for her. I will always weep for her!

Few towns have occupations where death is sure in times of war, as our little town has lived with death as long as I can remember. Neighbors, friends, coworkers, and families live with the occupational hazard of dying. Suddenly, and without warning, another citizen is taken in a faraway land. These deaths are commemorated by trees—Warriors Walk is now lined in multiple sections of far too many trees.

20) Freedom on The Fourth of July – 1976

We were excited about the upcoming 4th of July holiday. Saltwater, sand, and beer highlighted by fireworks and fried shrimp—a coastal Georgia ritual for as long as I can remember. But this was a special year, a bicentennial year—1976. This was about celebrating freedom! What could be better than a camping weekend on St. Catherine's Island with fifty of your best friends? Truly, the anticipation was not the smell of frying bacon over a campfire, crawling into a sleeping bag, or calling upon camping skills learned from days in the Boy Scouts. Nope, none of the above! The excitement was a weekend of partying on a virtually uninhabited island in the lazy, hazy, crazy days of summer, 70s style...if you get my drift. A true celebration of freedom!

Boatloads of twenty somethings hit the beach between McQueen's Inlet and the north end of St. Catherine's late afternoon on Sunday, July 4th, 1976. The bright full moon had not yet made its appearance, nor had the horrendous storms that would later blast the barrier islands off the Georgia coast. Oblivious and full of gaiety, the party started as more landings occurred with revelers arriving in waves. Gregg Allman's "All My Friends" theme was in play on this day, 1976, as the Allman Brothers Band was kicking it all weekend. Ironically, forty years later, Gregg would choose to live nearby.

Radios were dialed in sync to the same station, as each makeshift campsite, up and down the beach, kept the Allman Brothers near with their often-played beats. A beautiful afternoon in a beautiful place with your best buds, a buzz, and constant laughter made for an Independence Day to remember, and as it turned out, it certainly was!

Food did not play a prominent role in this setting, but the smell of cooking burgers (beach style) added to the atmosphere of the greatest family reunion ever! This was about FREEDOM, and offshore, no cars, no law, and no restrictions, we all felt free—young, half-hippie, 60s refugees with one central theme: have a blast! I've often thought about that afternoon, and its central theme: have a blast! A fifty-year look back now reveals strengths and weaknesses of that age and time. The weaknesses were what they were—immaturity and frivolity. The strength was the agreement with all present to put aside problems for a brief period and enjoy the setting, the people, the mood, the time—have a blast!

Ironically, I now live this way (almost all of the time); it's called Kingdom life, and I've learned it from my Heavenly Father.

The high sand dunes overlooking the Atlantic became a playground of sorts as a rough, somewhat bloody childhood game of King of the Hill broke out. Obviously, the girls questioned our sanity, but from our high vantage point atop the dunes, overlooking the beautiful beach and Atlantic, we all felt like kings. In what seemed liked minutes (instead of hours), night descended upon us, and the most beautiful ocean moon made its presence known. The mood changed to one of wonder, as the moonlight illuminated the dunes under our feet. It was so bright that we joked about getting a moon tan. Was it the substance within us or an accurate view of serene scenery? The reflection was like being on another planet—probably both!

Laughter was everywhere. Heck, it was the 200-year anniversary of our country, and we were celebrating in a safe, obscure way, out-of-the-way, but celebrating, having the time of our lives—full of confidence that these times would never end. Life was good.

We knew we had neighbors on Ossabaw, some older folks who wanted to be a little north of St. Catherine's on this special night. We planned a visit a little later, a short hop across the sound. They were nestled within the cabin of a beached shrimp boat—a perfect enclosure for camping, partying "coasties" who didn't want to deal with a tent.

What is that I hear? An interruption to the party? Is that distant thunder behind us? The sky lit up with customary summer lightning, but this was something else altogether. More like a coming storm, and before we knew it, a granddaddy of coastal storms was upon us, creeping up from the west, hidden by the front side of the island. Before our less than sharp minds could figure, we were in a violent summer storm. Immediately, we became concerned about our neighbors, and soon our less than sharp minds decided to cross St. Catherine's sound to check on our friends. A storm crossing in a small boat, in the middle of a lightning storm, is memorable, I promise! And stupid!

This storm was chronicled by the *Liberty County Herald*, who had reporter on site all weekend to report the occasion, or what of it was reportable. I have included their report here.

Upon arriving on Ossabaw, the unprotected boats of our neighbors were clanging together as the storm lashed the island and their boats anchored just offshore. We attempted to anchor them farther apart with very little success as the storm's rage kept us at bay. We ended up riding out the storm in the hull of that old shrimp boat, even enjoying a warm fire with rain pouring outside.

When the storm let up, we crossed back over to St. Catherine's where all were safe. As suddenly as it started, it stopped, as summer storms go on the coast.

In conclusion, our bicentennial celebration was large. We hope our founders are proud, not of our behavior so much, but of our celebration of the freedom this country has provided. It was freedom, the likes of which we must never take for granted, and a 200-year celebration of a not perfect, but still great, country.

On Ossabaw Island

Heavy Winds, Rain Strand Citizens

Approximately 30 Liberty countians were stranded on Ossabaw Island July 4 when a storm came tearing from the mainland swamping two boats and nearly sinking two others. The boats sunk belonged to Jimmy McLean of Hinesville and J. W. Morgan of Sunbury. The strong winds reportedly blew Morgan's boat into the McLean boat.

Over 60 people were on the beach at Ossabaw Island during the day of July 4 but many decided to make a run across the St. Catherines sound during the storm. Luckily, no serious injuries were reported.

The 30 citizens stranded on Ossabaw, men, women, and children, stayed the night in the old shrimp boat beached on the south end of Ossabaw. The Coast Guard couldn't rescue the large group due to the heavy winds and rain that occurred during the afternoon and night. All were safely returned to the mainland the following day.

The storm apparently hit sometime in the late afternoon moving from Hinesville, where strong winds were reported. From McIntosh to Midway several large trees were blown down from the strong Fourth of July winds, some narrowly missing homes. Again, no injuries were reported.

Other reports of trees downed by the high winds came from Fleming, Sunbury and Riceboro.

21) The Corner Bar

The Corner Bar at Midway was almost legendary in its day (1970s). She was brought to life and perpetuated by several local men, almost legends themselves: Jimmy Smith, listed in the local telephone book as "The Original One," and Rodney C (Elrod) Riley. Many notables from various walks performed their magic here. The songwriter of "The Dance," a Garth Brooks hit, played here as did many others. James Woods, of Hollywood fame, loved the atmosphere. It was a melting pot of rich and poor, black and white, young and old.

In this picture, you can see a future County Commission Chairman, Mayor Pro Tem, State Representative, US Army Helicopter Captain (Vietnam Combat veteran), and a Solar man. Society, color, and politics had no walls at The Corner Bar. There were no Republicans or Democrats at The Corner Bar. Men and women from many other South Georgia counties gathered here, many new friends made, and perhaps a romance or two spawned inside these walls.

Other less mentionable things happened here too, as the old landmark has faded in all but the memories of a few local men and women. Shrimpers, crabbers, fishermen, lawyers, doctors, bankers, and a few smugglers rubbed elbows here, turned up their glasses and mugs together singing "Seminole Wind" and "Swinging" with Leonard Beasly at the jukebox. The loud leaky window unit kept us cool while we sipped beer laced with ice giblets from a frosty mug. The smell was always the same, musky, but clearly familiar: The Corner Bar. We loved it!

Local musicians played their tunes on Saturday night. Songs we all loved, and one New Year's Eve, they all played, giving birth to the most talented local group ever: The Midway Allstars. The place was packed that night as friends from all over the coast gathered to welcome in the new year. Rowdy, raucous, and reckless were the 70s, and The Corner caught it, captured, and bottled it for us all to drink, and we did!

A local watering hole with a church-like quality. A bunch of people who really enjoyed each other. Should I use the word "love" here? Yeah, I will, as some of these people are still my dearest friends!

The old building is gone, but the memories live on. I laugh, often out loud, when I daily pass The Corner, the one at Highway 17 and 84 in Midway, Georgia.

22) Almost Famous on
St. Catherine's Island

A long time back, I received a phone call about going to St. Catherine's Island to take some pictures. Not unusual for the times, but in this case, most unusual. You see, this time there would be precious cargo onboard and a certain need to get there and back in one piece— not normally a requirement when going to the beach on St. Catherine's.

Ed Spivia, then Georgia's state film director, with whom I'd worked on numerous film projects, carefully explained that the guys involved liked to party and he needed my help to get them there and keep the raucousness to a minimum.

Sure thing, Ed, I thought...though I knew no details.

I was soon to receive another call from yet another part of this mystery train, as I was instructed to be on standby. No cell phones in those days. As promised, ring, ring. I answered, not really sure who I was about to speak with. When he said, "This is Phil Walden, President of Capricorn Records," I knew exactly who was on the other end of the line—career builder of Otis Redding (my all-time favorite R&B singer), the Allman Brothers Band (my favorite band ever), Marshall Tucker Band, Delaney & Bonnie, Wet Willy, Elvin Bishop, and many others.

Ed had provided details to Phil who graciously filled in the blanks as to exactly what was going on and what was needed. Music aficionados will remember the Allman Brothers split up when Gregg Allman testified against a roadie to save his butt in a drug trial. Chuck Leavell, the keyboard player, Jamio the drummer, and the base player, Lamar Williams, left the Allman Brothers to begin a new band, Sea Level. This was their first effort beyond the Allman Brothers, a pretty big deal carrying great expectations. The album cover was to be shot at sea level—St. Catherine's. Perfect!

With a little time to put things together, I amassed a great local crew to help keep the partying down: Eddie Burke, Nicky Clark, Len Holman, and Joe Underwood, all great mates for such a task. Just like myself, these guys were skilled in anti-party warfare.

I've seen many sights under the oaks at Yellow Bluff Fish Camp, but this day I would see a new one for sure, when up pulled a stretch limo with the band all dressed in Nero suits. I must tell you, Arthur (Goodman), the fish camp owner, was not impressed!

Before we reached the dock for the boat, somebody was smoking a funny cigarette, and cold beer flowed from Arthur's cooler to somebody else's. Also onboard was an Israeli photographer who took a million Polaroids before taking any with his fancy album cover camera. The day was shaping up to be very interesting...and a little fun!

Back then, the cut between Bird Island and the beach was pretty deep and easy to navigate, so we shot down the beach south until finding suitable dunes for the shoot. Everybody was festive and a bit excited—a beautiful St. Catherine's day added to the moment. We soon found a spot and unloading began, but so did the dreaded partying! My team and I were very frustrated and pressed into service...we were overcome by smoke and huddled briefly to decide what to do. We found our answer quickly—join them! And we did, and a good (no, great) time was had by all!

The album cover was shot, and the dunes of St. Catherine's were immortalized in music history, serving as the first cover for Sea Level. My name even made it onto the album. By the way, the Allmans later reunited, and Chuck Leavell found fame and fortune as the keyboardist and musical director for an English band: The Rolling Stones. What a day!

23) Marijuana on the Georgia Coast

In the mid-fifties, evening newscaster Walter Cronkite reported that "beatniks all over were now smoking marijuana."

"What is marijuana?" I asked my mom.

"It's a horrible drug that will make you crazy if you smoke it," she replied. As a small boy, I knew I would never be one of those beatnik people "'cause they were crazy!"

Fast forward ten years, Walter Cronkite again tells us, "Strange acting hippies are now occupying a spot in San Francisco (Haight-Ashbury), smoking the dangerous drug, marijuana." As in the fifties, these reports flowed into our living room almost nightly. Again I thought, "I don't want to be around none of those hippies."

I didn't cut it in high school, so summer school 1966 at South Georgia College was my only route into formal education. Typically, summer in Douglas was not much different than high school life with one major exception: The faces were different, the people and lifestyles far different from cozy little Hinesville, Georgia. Being a bit of a party boy who enjoyed a cold beer, I joined some of my new friends at a late afternoon bonfire in nearby woods. The radio was blasting top tunes as we sat in a circle around a fire not needed in summer, but I was new to college life, and I'd do what they were doing, sitz around an unneeded fire and sip my beer.

Just as things loosened a bit, this pretty girl with long blond hair (like Mary in Peter, Paul, and Mary), lit what looked like a hand-rolled, funny smelling cigarette. She puffed it pretty hard, shook that long shinny hair and handed it to the guy next to her. The handoff kept happening around the campfire. I realized, at a point real soon, it was coming to me! This was the dreaded marijuana I heard so much about. Mama warned me to watch for this! Should I excuse myself for a fake bathroom call, or just leave outright?

These people are hippies, I thought. Of all people to get hooked to in my first few days of college, I landed in the middle of this crowd. Heck, they all seemed nice enough, didn't seem crazy at all, and the blonde was pretty as a peach, very nice, and shook her hair like Mary. Now, I was a tad confused! Go or stay?

Fast forward again, 1975, marijuana smuggling reached its zenith off the Georgia Coast, a sanctuary for smugglers with its many rivers, creeks, tributaries, hidden marshes, high banks, and more importantly, many starving fisherman and shrimpers who knew these inlets like the back of their hand. It began when daring pilots would do the round trip to Columbia, South America and drop bales of pot in fields, swamps, highways—anywhere an undetected drop could be made—in Coastal Georgia. Soon the FAA and DEA were onto the plane traffic and slowed this import business to a halt. Boats and the high seas were the next battleground as Columbian ships anchored offshore and offloaded their bulky cargo to eager Americans who delivered to a pre-designated riverbank or dock on the Georgia Coast. From there, big trucks would dart in from I-95 for distribution up and down the coast. Liberty and McIntosh Counties were prime spots for smuggling due to the rural nature of the area and undeveloped barrier islands.

This cat and mouse game was played for several red-hot years in the mid to late 70s. I had friends on both sides of this highly illegal business. You see, my daddy was sheriff, whose job it was to shut down illegal activity, yet I had life-long friends who were up to their eyeballs in the trade. It was truly a strange time! I often detested being in a law enforcement family because of the blame and involvement we had with painful and often bad events in people's lives (I could write a whole other story about the oddity of being a sheriff's son in a small town). This was the worst of all those law enforcement years because it was now friends who my daddy and his constituents were after.

What complicated this even more was my own discovery about marijuana—it wasn't what Walter Cronkite told us; you see, I didn't leave that campfire back in the summer of 1966. My intrigue with the long blond hair held me captive, and I took my turn puffing the funny smelling cigarette. Nothing happened, so I kept sipping my beer. No one was yet crazy (secretly I had hoped to see how crazy the blonde would go). It came around again, I pulled harder on the weed, and still nothing crazy happened, nor to any of the others as far as I could see. It was sort of quiet except for the music, and then someone began laughing for no apparent reason, just laughing. Someone else also found humor and began laughing. That didn't seem all that crazy to me. Just laughing, and at what I didn't know! And then, I too found all this kind of funny. All these people laughing at really nothing. Before I knew it, I was laughing right along with them...freaking hilarious, I thought. I laughed until my stomach hurt, but at what? It seemed like time had slowed to a crawl. I'd been around this campfire forever, and these people, these people could be my friends forever!

So here is my daddy doing all he can to stop this evil weed, my friends trying to get it here, and me enjoying it when they did. Whose side was I on? Though I never participated in selling as much as a seed (out of respect for my daddy or knowingly doing something seriously criminal), I enjoyed smoking marijuana. It became part of normal life. We smoked at parties, after work, before workouts, and at home for relaxation. It was a normal baby boomer thing, just as normal as the evening cocktails in our parents' homes. It seemed to make food taste better, take the edge off, music popped, and movies were great if you could remember what you saw...and, it didn't make us go crazy or fight like liquor did. How confusing this all was.

I smoked from 1966 to Christmas Eve 1982. Without prior plans, notice, or hard conviction, I took a pull off a joint in the grease bay of a local filling station (remember that name—filling station?) and ended my pot and tobacco smoking days. I did not like what it was doing to my lungs or memory. Nobody believed I'd quit them both for good, but I did!

The picture shown here was taken in Green's Pasture, also known as Laurel View, not far from Sunbury. My dad, Sheriff Bobby Sikes on the right, and Harry Coursey (GBI) on left. These men and many others found this twenty tons of pot on a high bank in coastal Liberty County. After many days of staking it out, no one showed to take it to market, but one old crabber spied it from the river while running his traps. Without knowledge of being under high surveillance with all the latest electronic equipment, he crept forward and grabbed a single bale, covered it in his old crab boat and continued down the river. Pulling traps is hot and tiring work, and as the crabber proceeded to his next trap the ache and pain of the hard work probably induced him to spin the boat around for another catch (another bale), as each would fetch high dollars on the local market. When confronted at the local seafood dock by my dad, local DA, and GBI, the old crabber quick wittingly said, "Sheriff, look what I found for you out on the river!"

24) A Million Dollar Night
at Maxwellton Plantation

I graduated from Georgia Southern in 1971. There was much talk of getting football started again after being discontinued during WWII. In the few short years following graduation, the talk of a football program escalated as then college President Dale Lick linked with key leaders in Bulloch and surrounding counties and key educators within the university system. The one continuous roadblock was money. As contributions began to flow, President Lick and others hosted fundraisers throughout South Georgia. The need for a big named coach was key to raising money—people wanted a winner!

Football is a rich tradition in South Georgia, and Georgia Southern was the perfect place for the area's rich talent to find a home after high school. Many graduates of Southern and former high school players got behind this effort, and soon, University of Georgia's legendary defensive coach, Erk Russell, was recruited to head the effort, and lead it he did, bringing three NCAA Division 1-AA championships to Statesboro. He produced the first 15-0 team of the 20th century, inducted into the Georgia and Alabama Sports Hall of Fame, USA Today's Georgia Coach of the Year and Coach of the Decade in 1989. His legend lives on.

The photo above was taken on Maxwellton Plantation in what is now my backyard. In the picture are Coach Erk Russell, educator Waldo Pafford, me, and Professor Harris Mobley. This photo was taken in late 70s, and everyone is smiling—Liberty County came up big that night (over $1 million raised or committed at this event). The night was so successful, at one point, Coach Russell suggested naming the field Liberty Field for the support he received from our own, Liberty County. Many will remember the field that now houses the stadium was named "Bryant Field," so named for the generous gift provided by Glenn E. Bryant, a local businessman. Many factors came together to create Georgia Southern football, but none any greater than the night the light turned green with money from the Liberty County coast.

25) A White Christmas Speaks

The snow was falling, silent and beautiful, accumulating in an uncommon fashion. A winter wonderland in South Georgia—who could believe such a thing here at Christmas? The weatherman predicted it, yet as with many false predictions from times past, I faintly believed him. Yet now it was happening, almost without warning, snow swirling and sticking on leaves, tree limbs, and the semi-frozen ground.

Life was hard in these years, raising two boys as a single parent with very little money or much to celebrate, but snow at Christmas erased my low spirits with an excitement I hadn't felt in a long time.

I took up my spot on a low hanging limb about a mile from my house—an easy walk for a morning hunt on a cold December morning. As I sat, the first of the heavy snow came swirling—a real treat stemming from such a rare occurrence. I left the house for a chilly walk in the woods, my granddaddy's old Remington 12-gauge under my arm. Nothing was different about this walk; I made it and similar treks many times. I hunted these woods more than any other because I always lived in or near them from earliest childhood, yet this snowfall and subsequent accumulation changed everything—a changing landscape right before my eyes. My friends further north see this frequently, but for me, a South Georgia boy, a mesmerizing occasion. I was fascinated that change in appearance could happen so fast.

My hunting interest fell to my weather interest, and soon, I was wandering through the woods to clearings and fields to catch the white wonder, so pure and clean—a changing landscape from all I had ever known. The silence amidst such movement was also new to me. How could so much movement and change take place in total silence?

Amazing, I thought.

That morning is still alive in me. It represented a factor that would mark my life: change. Change from the traditional (what I'd always seen to a landscape I'd never seen—all from the same spot). Could it be that life offers so much change without changing much? Now, after almost fifty years of working within 250 feet of where I started, I realize the prophetic truth of that Christmas snow; yes, things can change immensely almost in kaleidoscope fashion: people, businesses, furniture, offices, degrees of failure and success, age, aspirations, health, and life, yet in many ways, remain the same. All amidst the silence of change. All from the same spot.

26) Enlightened by Darkness

I never saw it coming—a well-timed left hook caught my right temple and black was all I saw! Straining to open my eyes, I slowly regained knowledge of my surroundings, the fact that I had been sparring with a seasoned fighter, and that I had been hit very hard (though still conscious). I was not new to taking hard hits from sports and motorcycle racing but was very new to this blackness with opened eyes. Boxing is a dangerous sport, as just months earlier (November 1982) boxer Ray Mancini killed a man on live television.

Stunned, I asked a nearby friend if my eyes were opened or shut, realizing my worse fear when the answer came: "Opened!" I already knew they were. My eyes were opened, yet I could not see—a terrifying sensation! This scary moment was followed by a trip to the emergency room. Fear truly gripped me as we traveled to the nearby hospital, my mind racing and heart pounding with emotion. My body shook as I contemplated a life without sight.

Many things pass through your mind when facing blindness. It is overwhelming to say the least. I was not aware of the temporary nature of such injuries, nor had I ever experienced anything close to losing my sight, so fear, blame, anger, and sadness engulfed me at once. Why had I not used a safety helmet? Why fight such an experienced fighter? Why did he unload on me like that?

During that period of life, I constantly found myself in impossible situations of my own doing—always pushing myself, proving myself, but why? Taking huge risks had been my proving ground as a young adult, but now I was about to pay a great price for such nonsense. I had paid this price financially for similar high-risk business ventures, as with other areas of life, and now my stupidity had written a check my butt couldn't cash.

I felt like crying, and would have, but hell, I had an image to maintain: a tough guy can take it! As awkward and painful as those thirty or forty minutes were, they served me well. You see, I saw something that my temporarily blind eyes had never seen—I was trying to prove myself to me. Deep inside, I felt inadequate, not good enough, fearing failure more than death. My need to prove I was good enough in multiple arenas was my constant challenge, yet now I clearly saw the foolishness of this line of thought. Why had it taken such trauma to awaken me to this major flaw in my character?

A left hook straightened my senses, as that event changed much about me moving forward. I suddenly became much more satisfied, losing the insatiable desire to constantly prove myself. I found an inner peace in my blindness that literally and figuratively opened my eyes.

When my sight returned, a deeper perspective and self-image returned with it. My risk-taking wasn't over, but well on its way to being over. My blind fight with myself was also in its waning stages of existence, as temporary blindness introduced clear sight to something that had escaped me up to that point: becoming a mature man.

27) Good for Evil −1982

I had a temper, a bad one that exploded when I felt someone had wronged me. At age thirty-four, an older man took advantage of me on a real estate transaction. Predictably, I erupted, and though no physical violence occurred, I cussed him bad in front of his wife (who was a Christian). She began to pray for me.

Several days later, a police officer and friend saw pain in me and knew what I needed. He asked that I pray with him, as many things were going wrong in my life. That simple prayer changed me forever—the rage and anger that had such a grip practically disappeared. My heart was changed, and love replaced hate. I now had something I'd never known: a personal relationship with my savior.

Several months passed, but one particular afternoon, I felt an enormous love for the man who had wronged me. I knew I had to find him and humbly apologize for my actions. Though he had done me wrong, for some reason, that no longer mattered; what mattered now was apologizing for my foul behavior. I found him, and with his wife's help, a meeting was set. I was shaking when I entered his home, and tears flowed from my eyes. I apologized—it was an earnest, heartfelt apology. The gentleman accepted my apology but quickly clarified that this apology changed nothing about the real estate deal. I didn't go there with that expectation, yet when I left his home, I felt free. I felt like I'd never felt before.

A year passed, and this same gentleman contacted me about discussing some business. As it turned out, I was needed again to bring this real estate opportunity to fruition. I gladly got back on board and quickly brought the deal to completion. I was paid my full brokerage fee, and the gentleman received the large sum of money he needed.

Twenty-three years later, the buyer, who built a major shopping center on the property, offered to sell me the shopping center at a very favorable price and terms. I was stunned to say the least but was able to acquire the center and two more. On the day of the closing, as I entered the attorney's office, the Holy Spirit spoke clearly saying, "To those who will follow my instruction in returning good for evil, I will cause you to inherit a blessing—a blessing without sorrow, a blessing for all time."

To this day, our shopping centers provide income in our older age, provide a living for eight families, and bless us with much satisfaction. It is the gift that keeps on giving. What a lesson for a hard head like me: return good for evil and watch God do something great in your life! You can argue a man's doctrine until you are blue in the face, but you cannot argue his testimony.

Thank you, Dickie Welch, for leading me to the Lord.

28) The Shed

The silence of the chilly predawn hour was broken with awakening voices heard all about the encampment around "The Shed." The smell of frying sausage and bacon blanketed the air, enticing us all to a big country breakfast. The Shed, the island scene of food and gathering for fifty years, was once again casting its mystical spell on hunters from far and wide for yet another year of passionate deer hunting. This mythical structure drew us into an annual family-like setting, welcoming us home from a long journey. Set perfectly on a salt riverbank, its backdrop always produced a spectacular setting, miles of massive marshes and salt rivers fed by the nearby Atlantic Ocean. Sunrise over St. Catherine's, a nearby barrier island, produced a spectacle of light seldom seen by most humans.

The Shed was a tradition as rich as Christmas for many men and their sons, as this morning was the one event that comes but once a year, the Liberty County Sheriff's hunt with its rich tradition of fun and fellowship, young and old alike. I'd known The Shed since earliest memory; it was my friend and happy place all rolled into one. Even when I'd see it standing empty, when no crowds surrounded it, I smiled as memories of fond joy flooded my heart. The Shed represented the love of my father, his love of fellowship and friends, and endless laughter as I've never seen before or since. The memory is etched deep!

This morning, The Shed brought us together in annual reunion, warming us with a cedar log crackling fire, feeding our hungry stomachs with breakfast made by Pompey and Douse, two black men whose cheese eggs, cheese grits, country cured bacon and sausage readied us for a long day. Nobody cooked a breakfast like these two beloved men. What a treat to pick them up each year for this great occasion. These annual hunts were a highlight of my younger years, from child to middle-aged adult. These people, many of whom I saw but once a year, became more family than friend. Years later, I sobbed uncontrollably when I learned of Pompey's death.

In other uses, The Shed became the Thursday afternoon spot to be, as Hinesville shut all businesses on Thursday at lunch, its men coming to the coast for the cool breeze and weekly suppers hosted by my daddy and his friends. Law enforcement from as many as five counties would make these suppers of squirrel, chitlins, fish, shrimp, deer, goat, but most consistently, seafood caught the day of the supper. We would seine on nearby St. Catherine's and Ossabaw, cast for mullet and shrimp, shoot squirrels in season, always seeking something fresh to cook. My uncle, Walter (Zech) Zechman, often did the cooking, a master chef by our calculations, whose roar of laughter became his trademark; in fact, my standout memory of The Shed is laughter. Nobody laughed like Tom and Carole Smith, our cousins, Zech, my uncle, and my daddy, Bobby Sikes. Throw in a Theron Rogers, Hub Swindell, Luther Groover, Freeman Smith, Frank Bagley, Jack Keel, and many others, and a symphony of sound occurred—happiness and joy produce a sound; it's called laughter!

Whether the annual hunts or the weekly gatherings, The Shed offered its ambience and welcoming smile to us all—hallowed ground to those who lived in the 60s, 70s, and 80s in Liberty County, Georgia. Many parties and victory celebrations took place here, political rallies, and fundraisers. More than one governor launched their South Georgia bid to lead the state here, as did US Congressmen who led our district. The Shed has hosted luminaries from both sports and film, wealthy to poor, and black and white have broken bred together under The Shed.

With passing time, as with all mentioned above, The Shed is gone, yet remains strong in my memory. To remember the laughter makes me laugh, even to this late day in my life. You see, precious memories like this never leave, but most especially with what remains of The Shed, now rest in my front yard, nearest where I sleep every night. When morning comes, I can throw back the curtain, cast a glance to that special corner, and relive the times of my life!

29) The Old Sunbury Road

There is not much left of this old road, one of the oldest, most historic in our state, once connecting the port town of Sunbury (and its 94 port vessels) to the state's capital in Milledgville. If this old road could talk, the stories it could tell, back to its origins as an Indian trail to its most traveled times connecting coastal settlers to the inland. Even in the modern era, there are tall tales involving drug smugglers, adoring lovers, recreational hunters, and moonshine runners. The span and the history of this road are as rich as it gets in the USA, as this passageway connected island and coastal Indians with trade opportunities to tribes farther north. Even today, non-indigenous flint rock arrowheads and other artifacts can be found on or near this road after a hard rain.

The routes we travel today often began with Native Americans who searched the high ground, forged the streams, establishing the least difficult river passages. These trails transcended into much traveled roadways for settlers with horses and wagons, and yes, an occasional horseshoe or wagon part can still be found with today's metal detecting technology. This road, known as "The Old Sunbury Road," is fronted by one of the nation's oldest cemeteries, filled with names found in history books. Many are unaware that Sunbury is now known as a "Dead Town" but once rivaled Savannah as the major seaport in this area. By all geological rights, it should have been what Savannah became; after all, it is the deepest natural harbor east of the Mississippi. It has direct access to the ocean with its necessary winds, much shorter to get to from the high seas, while Savannah offered only a winding, often difficult silted river to navigate.

General James B. Vault, a former Ft. Stewart commander and military planner, and also a friend prior to his death, did his war college dissertation on why such a natural harbor (Sunbury) was bypassed—his findings, though I never read it, were interesting! As the story goes, in the early days, loyalty to the crown played a big role in how decisions were made. Apparently, St. John's Parrish (later named Liberty County) held a dim view of crown rule, which may hold some truth as evidenced by the number of signers of the Declaration of Independence who lived here. Disloyalty to those in power meant a lack of favor from the powerful—in this case, the crown. My how things have changed!

The historic markers at Sunbury will whet your appetite, as you will soon realize you are sitting on one of the most historic pieces of real estate "per square inch" in this country. While the paved roads will allow you to easily find Sunbury (you must try Sunbury Crab Company if you go), it is that old dirt road you will want to leave by. It will eventually guide you back to Hwy 38, but take it, and take your imagination with you. I promise that you won't be disappointed.

30) The Day the Music Died (On the Georgia Coast)

It was 1959. I heard a sound coming from downstairs—music I hadn't heard. Sure didn't sound like Perry Como, Dean Martin, Frank Sinatra, or the Tommy Dorsey Band, those parental choices I was forced to listen to, so who was making this sound? This got my attention! A black woman, a soulful, gifted black woman: Mahalia Jackson, so rich and soulful, at what I later learned was gospel.

This absolutely breathtaking music sounded like what I heard at black funerals: music that drew me in, caught my attention, and moved my soul. I liked it and played it over and over when my parents were gone. Then, Daddy brought home another one, Ray Charles, and I loved him even more, as it too had a soulful wisp, like singing from deep within a pained heart. I wore these records out until I heard Sam Cooke on the radio; Jackie Wilson and Motown changed everything! Imagine that, white kids drawn to black music in the late 50s and well into the 60s. I never got any criticism for it, but my St. Simons grandmother preferred I listen to her collection of classical music. I wanted to be respectful, but that was asking a little too much!

Music had just begun to affect me, as the sound I was seeking was definitely black music of sorts, or at least had roots in this culture. Elvis touched it a little, Eric Burton of the Animals getting close, but nobody else, including the Stones, could match what we really wanted. Otis Redding out of Macon "lit it up" for a bit but died in a plane crash; Janis Joplan found it and lost it with a drug overdose, and with the exception of Sam and Dave, Jackie Wilson, The Temptations, The Four Tops, Marvin Gaye, and James Brown, nothing much else was shaking this music in a real way for many of us *until* we heard a cut of the Allman Brothers Band.

Around 1970, everything changed again! White boys were touching a real blues sound. Clean, crisp, clear, raw, and somewhat uncensored—long bluesy slide guitar runs (often extraordinary), always complimented with that raw boned, soulful Gregg Allman voice: great guitar riffs, but the raw singing white boy was like nothing heard at this point in time. How can a young man sing like that? This is exactly what we are looking for: a white group who could bring it with a blues sound, yet rock, truly rock—rocking it with a soulful sound that became a unique genre of music: southern rock!

King David states in the Bible that every generation has a unique sound assigned to that specific generation, and ours was tied to something jazzy, country, soulful, bluesy, that rocked; hence the birth of southern rock, performed by the Allman Brothers Band, whose pained, strained voices were real from the tragedy that struck them early. This would pave the way for Lynard Skynard and Marshall Tucker, and others, but they would all play "catch up" to ABB, masters of the blues sound due in large part to the voice of Gregg and the slide guitar of Duane Allman and Dickie Betts.

Through the years, I would return to this music over and over again, and be blessed to find others who carry on the tradition; Mike Farris, St Paul and The Broken Bones, Tedeshi Trucks, Nathaniel Radcliffe and the Night Sweats, John Fulbright, Government Mule, and many, many others keep me up late some nights, but I love it still!

Gregg was an icon, a true memorial to his genre, having sprung many new groups who hit the southern rock groove in steady fashion. Not only a founding father of the Allman Brothers Band, but also a father figure to a whole new generation of blues rockers, who pitch a little southern into it for true authenticity.

Gregg took his last breath right here on the Georgia Coast in his beautiful home on the Belfast River. He could have lived anywhere, but he chose to live here among us. He is sorely missed, but his spirit lives on through his music, "and the road goes on forever."

31) It's Not All Black and White (Here on the Coast)

He and I don't see eye-to-eye...never have! His perspectives and mine are light-years apart; we argue, debate, reason, and disagree—always have! Since age seven or eight, a relationship began with a wrestling match to see who the best fighter was, and we bonded.

He washed dishes at my grandmother's motel in Midway, where it all started, continuing through high school, the Civil Rights Movement, threats against us, college years, military service and Vietnam for him, later in business, politics, a wedding, and now a long-lived life. Through it all, the bond never failed us.

I was his best man in the 70s, which made some of his people mad. He was my business partner in the same period, which made some of my people mad. The differences then seemed hard to work through, but truth is, even harder today!

How can two people so different stay in the same room: one African American the other white, one liberal Democrat the other conservative Republican, both with intensely strong views, diametrically opposite beliefs?

I've written about our differences over the years but also what trumps the separation: our love and respect for each other, and ultimately the respect that we hold for the other's perspective. Maybe not understood, but nevertheless respected.

In today's world, we are deeply divided—perspectives are vastly different. One sees the glass half full, the other half empty—both see the same glass, but interpret what they see from past experiences, personal understanding, and present circumstance.

My view may not align with yours, or then again it might; the key issue is *forbearance* to allow my perspective, as I too do the same for you. We can actually care a great deal for each other while holding different views.

Different views should never mean enemy, outcast, or rogue. It should mean my friend, Al Williams, and I can hold intensely different perspectives while allowing the bond of love and trust to unite us in lifelong friendship, very rich fellowship, and perhaps an ability to see from another's point of view.

Today again, we debated—he didn't change my mind, nor did I change his, but again, we laughed, shook hands, and marveled at the wonderful years God has given us together.

* The Bond: A force much greater than hate, divisiveness, disagreement, misunderstanding, etc. A power within that overrides every force that divides. The bond of love is much greater.

32) Full Moon on the Beach

Walking on the beach tonight, just like when I was young.

The moon is full tonight; its light dancing on the ocean sparkling like diamonds, and the warm southeast wind invigorates the comfort of it all.

I hear the faint sound of voices in the distance—others enjoying this evening enchantment.

The dunes are filled with lovers tonight, just like when I was young!

33) My Dock

The early evening sounds of a whippoorwill announce the night, and the marsh hen's cackle settles and fades. The long day has ended, yet the night begins afresh with a full moon and tide.

Island nights on the Georgia coast tempered by flowing moss from gentle breezes and non-existent darkness when the big moon arrives. You can see for miles, and the stars shine so bright that they twinkle. The whine of a boat in the ICW, buoys dancing for miles, dock lights from a nearby island, and suddenly the splash of a fish in the water underneath.

Let me take this all in, enjoy my remaining years on this dock, this place where sounds are like music and sights like sparkles from heaven.

There is but one time and place I relish solitude: my dock when the big moon and tide come.

34) The Peace of Night

The gentle breeze of a spring night blows through the pines as a full moon shines down on the South Georgia town. Cool air refreshes as I stand staring and listening to the night of Hinesville, Georgia. Every town has a unique sound. In Bellville, it's a train and wind of open space; in Hinesville, the crickets, passing trucks from a distant highway, and firing at Ft. Stewart. Always the same. For the entirety of my now long life, always the same, but never boring.

Why am I so mesmerized by the sights and sounds of the night, making distinguishing differences in the places I sleep? I honestly don't know. On St. Simons, it was the roar of the ocean, the sound of buoys and ships, and occasional laughter in the neighborhood. I could sit, listen, and stare for hours.

Now, I'm on an island, Colonel's Island, where the night sounds differ from any place I've lived—no trucks, guns, or trains. Just settling marsh hens, distant whippoorwills, and a soothing breeze rattling the palms. A quiet I've never known. An awesome, peaceful silence.

I love the night, enjoying all it has to offer. A place of rest, peace, and reflection: the end of the day, the quieting of my soul.

Peace.

35) The Wealth of Age

The most interesting aspect of aging is wisdom gleaned in the process. Not the least of which is when one chapter ends, another begins. Every sunset produces a sunrise.

God sees to it that what we lose in one arena is more than gained in another, yet even this requires the grace to receive fully. Prayer: the tool of the ages.